Getting Wise to Drugs

by the same authors

Understanding Drug Issues
A Photocopiable Resource Workbook
2nd edition
David Emmett and Graeme Nice
ISBN 978 1 84310 350 9

Understanding Street Drugs
A Handbook of Substance Misuse for Parents, Teachers and Other Professionals
2nd edition
David Emmett and Graeme Nice
ISBN 978 1 84310 351 6

of related interest

Contentious Issues
Discussion Stories for Young People
Márianna Csóti
ISBN 978 1 84310 033 1

Helping Children to Build Self-Esteem
A Photocopiable Activities Book
2nd edition
Deborah Plummer
Illustrated by Alice Harper
ISBN 978 1 84310 488 9

Self-Esteem Games for Children
Deborah Plummer
Illustrated by Jane Serrurier
ISBN 978 1 84310 424 7

Cool Connections with CBT
Encouraging Self-esteem, Resilience and Well-being in Children and Young People
Laurie Seiler
ISBN 978 1 84310 618 0

Working with Gangs and Young People
A Toolkit for Resolving Group Conflict
Jessie Feinstein and Nia Imani Kuumba
ISBN 978 1 84310 447 6

Social Awareness Skills for Children
Márianna Csóti
ISBN 978 1 84310 003 4

Getting Wise to Drugs

A Resource for Teaching Children about Drugs,
Dangerous Substances and Other Risky Situations

David Emmett and Graeme Nice

Jessica Kingsley Publishers
London and Philadelphia

First published in 2008
by Jessica Kingsley Publishers
116 Pentonville Road
London N1 9JB, UK
and
400 Market Street, Suite 400
Philadelphia, PA 19106, USA

www.jkp.com

Copyright © David Emmett and Graeme Nice 2008

Library of Congress Cataloging in Publication Data
A CIP catalog record for this book is available from the Library of Congress

British Library Cataloguing in Publication Data
A CIP catalogue record for this book is available from the British Library

ISBN 978 1 84310 507 7

Printed and bound in Great Britain by
Printwise (Haverhill) Ltd, Suffolk

To Mick Davies, Personal and Social Education Consultant, and valued friend, with grateful thanks for his invaluable advice during the preparation of this volume.

Contents

For 10–11-year-olds

Introduction

We have been closely involved in writing and presenting substance misuse and safety education to young people across a wide age range for more than 20 years. Throughout that time it has been apparent to us that simply telling young people 'don't take drugs', 'don't smoke', 'don't drink' or 'don't take risks' was not an effective way of delivering this type of education. Let us make our position on these issues crystal clear. We firmly believe that young people would be wise to steer clear of street drugs and tobacco, should, if they choose, learn to use alcohol in moderation, and have the necessary awareness to avoid unnecessary risk taking. In our work we have seen at first hand the often tragic consequences of young people's unwise involvement with such issues. However, it is not for us to tell them what to think or what to decide. It is for each young person to do that for themselves. If we were simply to advise them to do or not to do a certain thing, then all they have to do is to ignore this if they choose to do the opposite. If, on the other hand, we enable them to gain knowledge and greater understanding of many of the issues concerning such things as drug use, smoking, drinking and risk taking, they then have to reject all of that internalized knowledge and understanding if they still decide to get involved, a much more difficult task.

The past two decades or so have seen the establishment of many well thought out programmes of substance misuse education for post 11-year-old young people. During that same time frame, however, it has become apparent to us that the first involvement of young people with drugs, alcohol and smoking has begun to occur at younger and younger ages.[1] It is not an uncommon experience for us to listen to young people under the age of ten talking openly about their own and their friends' involvement in such activities. It is our view, therefore, that substance misuse education needs to be provided at an early stage in the lives of young people to provide them with the necessary knowledge and understanding, enabling them to make healthier choices. It is also our view that many of the issues surrounding young people and substance misuse are connected with 'making life more exciting', and as a result this book also seeks to provide education around the topics of risk taking, through exploration, risk recognition, assessment, reduction and, in appropriate circumstances, avoidance.

Early attempts at substance misuse prevention education depended very largely on the principle of 'shock horror'. Films were produced showing cancerous human lungs, festering drug injection sites, cirrhotic livers and so on. The simple idea was that such scenes could not fail to deter, thus preventing the problem arising. It soon became clear that this approach was failing or, at best, its effects were only short lived. Young people were indeed shocked and

---

1   McKeganey, N. *et al.* (2003) Preteen Children and Illegal Drugs. *Drugs: Education, Prevention and Policy 11*, 4, 315–327.

horrified but they were also fascinated. In some cases this fascination may even have led directly to experimentation. This is perhaps not surprising as young people believe themselves to be immortal and immune to the negative potential consequences of such actions.

Substance prevention education then moved to the information model. The simple idea was that if educators passed on information about such substances to young people then they would take the right decisions. The flaw in this approach was that, despite giving them all the necessary facts to make a decision, we failed to teach them how to handle the many different pressures that surround the total decision making process. Efforts were then made to rectify this flaw by adopting the 'just say no' approach, where fiercely negative messages were added so that young people were left with two clear choices, rejection of all that they had been taught, or rejection of substance misuse. Clearly, with the rapid escalation in young people's drug use over the last two or three decades this approach has also failed to a large extent.

In our view all involved in educating in this area should be fully aware of the possibility that young people with whom they are dealing may currently be experiencing or have previously been exposed to the negative consequences of substance misuse and risk within their family and social circles. It is therefore vital that in delivering this education we consider the highly sensitive and personal nature of these topics for such individuals.

New strategies must therefore be found and utilized whereby even very young people can become involved in their own education about these issues and their views sought, considered and valued. When the time comes for each young person to make a real life decision about their own involvement in drugs, alcohol, smoking or any other risky behaviour, it is unlikely that they will have a 'guardian angel' close by ready to tell them the best way to act. Instead, they will be making that decision on their own, often under powerful peer pressure. In our view the most effective way of helping them to make good choices is to provide them with both information and understanding of all of the possibilities that they need to consider.

Adrian King of the Drugs Education Forum, writing in 2004, advised that educators of young people should not treat drugs as an isolated issue.[2] Rather, drug education should be set in the wider context of the lives experienced by our young people. The authors of this volume agree totally and have set out to present a series of exercises that both challenge and provide information across a range of related topics. The primary focus remains that of substance misuse, but this is presented within a context of risk-taking behaviour in general.

At the end of the book, group leaders and teachers will find a list of useful organizations and websites, which offer further advice and guidance on the teaching of those issues covered by the exercises in this volume.

As in our previous workbooks, the exercises in this new volume are devised not to put young people down by telling them that they are wrong, bad or stupid if they become involved in smoking, drinking alcohol, misusing drugs or other risky behaviour. On the contrary they have been devised to allow them to explore and enhance their knowledge, and challenge their attitudes and beliefs about such issues, whilst at the same time encouraging them to look at these topics in a comprehensive and forward-looking manner, considering a whole range of possible outcomes.

2   King, A. (2004) *Advice for Teachers on Delivering Drug Education.* London: Drug Education Forum.

We recognize that levels of intellectual and social maturity vary widely and that we all deal with young people from the most 'street wise' to the most 'innocent'. It is our hope that by treating them in a responsible, respectful and intellectually appropriate manner, they will become enabled to make better informed decisions concerning their own actions.

This resource takes account of many learning styles and hopefully will cater for the majority rather than the few. Similarly, we have deliberately designed each exercise to be as flexible as possible in its presentation and use. Teachers will easily be able to adapt each exercise to suit their own teaching styles and the capabilities and needs of any particular group. We hope that these exercises will stimulate young people and, through awareness raising, go some way to reduce the numbers who experiment with substances or go on to develop greater problems.

Exercise 1

Full House

Suggested age: 8–9 • Suggested time: 40 minutes

Outline

An exercise consisting of 24 statements describing a personal experience of a safety related issue that participants have to match to other members of the group.

Purpose and expected outcome

- To demonstrate that personal experiences of health and safety situations are commonplace in everyday life.

- To enable participants to consider and explore the implications of such health and safety situations for the individual concerned and for others.

- To reinforce safety and healthy living messages.

Method

The exercise worksheet details 24 examples, divided between two worksheets, of health or safety situations that may have been experienced by members of the group. The teacher or group leader should distribute copies of either one or both worksheets, to individuals, pairs or small groups of participants, depending on the nature of the group and the time available. The group leader should explain that participants are to circulate amongst the rest of the group to locate others who have personal experience of one of the situations outlined in the worksheet. Their aim is to complete all the health and safety situations listed in the boxes on their worksheet by writing the relevant group member's first name in the appropriate space in each box. Participants should not write their own name in a box, even if they have experienced the particular situation. After the allotted maximum time for this part of the exercise, no more than 10–15 minutes, or once any participant has completed their worksheet and called 'full house', the group leader should bring the group back together to:

1. allow participants to calculate their worksheet score by counting their completed name boxes

2. allow selected participants to give greater details of, or answer questions from the group about, a personal experience of one of the issues and what effects it has had on them and others

3. encourage a general group discussion of the issues raised.

Notes for teacher or group leader

Teachers and group leaders should be sensitive to the possibility that some participants may be adversely affected by some statements. The group leader should use their judgement in dealing with the possibility that one participant may complete their sheet in such a short time that others in the group are unable to participate fully and meaningfully.

This exercise contains some words and expressions that may be unfamiliar to participants and require further explanation. These include the following:

- inhaler

- allergic

- food poisoning

- drugs.

Follow-up exercises

- Collect stories from newspapers or magazines that illustrate one or more of the types of scenarios outlined in the exercise about health and safety.

✓

1.1 Find someone...

...who uses
an inhaler

...who hates
cigarette
smoke

...who is
allergic to
something

...who has
tried beer

...who has
seen a
doctor in the
past month

...who has
broken a
bone

...who has
tried vodka
or
champagne

...who has
fallen off a
skateboard

...who has
had stitches
for a cut

...who has
tried wine

...who has
had
an injection

...who has
been stung
by a wasp

1.2 Find someone...

...who has fallen off a bicycle

...who has been bitten or scratched by an animal

...who has seen someone drunk

...who has cut themselves on broken glass

...who has had food poisoning

...who has fallen out of a tree

...who knows someone who smokes cigarettes

...who uses medicines every day

...who has found a needle and syringe

...who has fallen off a climbing frame or swing

...who has burnt themselves

...who knows someone who uses drugs

Exercise 2

Tell the Truth

Suggested age: 8–9 • Suggested time: 40 minutes

Outline

A quiz in 'true or false' and short answer format, designed to allow participants to check out their knowledge and understanding of substance misuse and other risky behaviours.

This quiz is the first of four, one for each age group, contained in this volume. A number of similar questions are to be found in some of the quizzes. This is deliberate and allows for the answers given by participants to become more comprehensive as their maturity and understanding develops.

Purpose and expected outcome

- To provide accurate information about drugs and drug use, alcohol use, smoking and other risky behaviour.

- To encourage thoughtful debate about such issues.

- To encourage good decision making.

- To reinforce safety and healthy living messages.

Method

The quiz consists of 35 questions designed to be suitable for young people aged eight to nine years. The first two sheets contain 15 questions each which all require answers of either 'true' or 'false'. The third sheet has five questions which require short paragraph-length answers. The teacher or group leader can decide on the length of the quiz to suit the participants and the time available.

It should be explained to the participants that the purpose of the quiz is not to examine their level of knowledge about such topics as drugs, alcohol, smoking and other forms of risky behaviour but rather to encourage them to consider such issues and check out the

accuracy or otherwise of any knowledge they may already have, and to add useful, accurate and balanced information.

The quiz sheets should be copied and handed out to the participants, and time allowed for them to answer the questions. The teacher or group leader should then go through the answers with the participants using the guidance notes below. Many of the questions will prompt discussion of the question itself and a number of associated issues. This is intended, and should be encouraged.

Participants should be asked to correct their sheets in line with the given answers and keep them for future reference.

Notes for teacher or group leader

This exercise contains some words and expressions that may be unfamiliar to participants and require further explanation. These include the following:

- addictive

- sniffing solvents

- drugs

- pedestrian crossing point.

Suggested answers

1. **True**. Whilst many drugs prescribed by a doctor can be very good for your health, there are many others that can be very harmful to your health, e.g. heroin, nicotine, cannabis, etc. It should be remembered that even medicinal drugs prescribed by the doctor can be harmful if misused.

2. **True**. Use of many drugs, including most of the illegal 'street' drugs, can lead to the user becoming addicted or dependent on them This dependence means that the craving for the drug can be very strong and abstaining from use of the drug can be very difficult.

3. **True**. Excessive alcohol use can lead to many health problems. Heart and liver disease, increased risks of strokes, stomach, liver and mouth cancer, and dementia are all associated with excess alcohol use.

4. **True**. Tobacco contains nicotine, a highly addictive stimulant drug.

5. **False**. When someone smokes tobacco, the air becomes contaminated with tobacco smoke over a wide area. This can be particularly thick when several people smoke in the same room. This smoke contains high levels of toxic chemicals and can lead even in the non-smoker to all of the diseases associated with smoking.

6. **False**. Sniffing solvents is *highly dangerous*. There is a danger of sudden death caused by overstimulation of the heart or asphyxiation caused by swelling of the throat tissues or inhalation of vomit. Users also expose themselves to a high level of accident risk whilst intoxicated.

7. **False**. Getting drunk on alcohol carries with it a high risk of serious accidents, especially when driving or operating machinery. It can be especially dangerous to young people who may become insensible very quickly with a high risk of asphyxiation due to inhalation of vomit. Young people in particular are at risk of alcohol poisoning.

8. **True**. Many addicted drug users spend large sums of money on their drugs of choice. For many such users this money is raised by theft, drug dealing or prostitution.

9. **False**. Tea, coffee and cola all contain caffeine, a mild stimulant drug. In small quantities it provides a refreshing increase in energy levels; in larger quantities it can lead to headaches, anxiety, agitation, tremors and insomnia. In extreme cases it has been known to cause death.

10. **True**. The breath, hair and clothing of smokers often smell very stale and unpleasant. Even being in the same room as someone who is smoking can make your hair and clothing smell in the same way.

11. **False**. Whilst excessive consumption of alcohol does lead some people to behave in an unthinking, careless, noisy or aggressive way, drinking in sensible, moderate amounts will not do this.

12. **True**. Smoking tobacco is one of the most common avoidable causes of illness and death in most countries.

13. **True**. Smokers rapidly become addicted to tobacco. They will smoke every day, seven days each week, 52 weeks each year. If a pack of cigarettes costs £5 and they smoke one pack every day then that habit will cost them £1825 each year and they will have nothing but ill health to show for it.

14. **True**. The tar in tobacco is deposited on the smoker's teeth, giving them a yellow colour.

15. **False**. Risk taking is a natural part of most young people's personality. Taking risks can be exciting and enjoyable and can enhance personal development. The important thing is to know the exact nature of the risk you are taking and what the possible drawbacks and benefits of taking it are.

16. **True**. As above. Also, circumstances may arise when it is necessary to take a risk to achieve something important, such as saving someone's life.

17. **True**. Skateboarding is a potentially risky sport. It is that risk that makes it so exciting. The level of risk to the skateboarder can be reduced by wearing a helmet and knee and elbow pads without making it less exciting.

18. **True**. Being struck by a motor vehicle kills many thousands of young people worldwide every year.

19. **True**. Many countries exempt certain people with certain medical conditions from the need to wear a seat belt in a car. Generally, however, most countries require the driver and passengers to wear correctly fitted seat belts.

20. **False**. If a bus or coach is involved in an accident, passengers can get thrown around violently inside the vehicle. They can even be thrown out of the vehicle. If seat belts are fitted they should always be worn.

21. **False**. Used sensibly, candles need not cause danger. However, they should never be left unsupervised and should only be used on fireproof surfaces and away from anything flammable.

22. **False**. Most medicines, if used incorrectly, have the potential to cause harm. This is particularly so when incorrectly used by young people. They should be kept out of reach of young people at all times.

23. **False**. The sale of fireworks is controlled in most countries, with an age limit often being applied. In the UK and in the USA it is illegal to sell fireworks to anyone under the age of 18. In 2004, in the UK, 1136 people were injured in firework accidents with 515 of them needing hospital treatment. More than half of these casualties were young people under the age of 18. In 2004, in the USA, 9600 people were treated for firework injuries in hospital emergency rooms.

24. **True**. They are also illegal. Whilst the emergency services are wasting time on a false call they can not be readily available to help someone who is genuinely in need of help.

25. **True**. The edges of broken glass can be razor sharp and cause serious injuries. Broken glass should never be left where other people can come into contact with it.

26. **False**. Whilst many wild mushrooms are both safe and delicious to eat, there are many highly poisonous varieties. Some of these poisonous varieties look very similar to edible ones.

27. **False**. In the UK you are not required to wear a helmet whilst cycling. However, should you fall or be knocked off your bike, wearing a helmet could save you from a potentially life-threatening head injury.

28. **False**. Besides being illegal, all such drugs carry health risks. They are often contaminated with other substances and of uncertain strength. The first-time user may suffer an unexpected adverse reaction to the drug or contaminating substance. Also, most illegal drugs carry the risk of addiction developing. *All* addicted drug users started with just one 'try'.

29. **True**. They may not be suitable for others and may lead to an adverse reaction.

30. **True**. We all have to take responsibility for ourselves. Others may well share that responsibility, especially when we are young.

Questions to think about

31. A single lit cigarette dropped in the wrong circumstances could set something else alight and thus start a small fire. That small fire could ignite something bigger, and so on until a major fire results. For example, a lit cigarette dropped on a chair with flammable foam cushioning could set fire to that chair. The burning chair could set fire to the whole house and lead to a large number of casualties.

32. Smoking cannabis can lead to loss of short-term memory, impaired judgement, dry mouth, lethargy, decreased blood pressure, bloodshot eyes, dizziness, confusion, anxiety, panic, paranoia, psychosis, depression, schizophrenia, and has a potential to cause cancers and breathing disorders. For many people the decision to start smoking cannabis is followed by the decision to use other, more dangerous, drugs.

33. Many illegal drugs are very impure, containing many contaminating substances. These substances may not dissolve completely and may lead to blockages of small blood vessels. Injecting drugs carries the risk of vein collapse and of infections such as HIV/AIDS and hepatitis, if injecting equipment is shared. Once a drug is injected it can not be removed from the body, thus any adverse reactions are potentially more dangerous.

34. Smoke alarms will sound long before the levels of smoke become dangerously high. This provides people with valuable time to evacuate a burning building. Many fires start at night when the occupants of a building are asleep. Smoke alarms will wake them and allow them to escape.

35. See answer 29.

Follow-up exercises

- The quiz will have raised many issues connected with risky behaviour. Any of these can be followed up with discussions, role-play exercises, story writing, or researching local and national newspapers and magazines.

2.1 Tell the Truth (1)

	True	False
1. Some drugs can be bad for you.	☐	☐
2. Some drugs can be addictive.	☐	☐
3. Too much alcohol can affect your health.	☐	☐
4. Tobacco contains an addictive drug.	☐	☐
5. Other people smoking cannot affect your health.	☐	☐
6. Sniffing solvents isn't very dangerous.	☐	☐
7. Getting drunk is fun and safe.	☐	☐
8. Some people steal to get money for illegal drugs.	☐	☐
9. The legal drug in tea, coffee and cola cannot harm anyone.	☐	☐
10. Cigarette smoke can make you smell.	☐	☐
11. Drinking alcohol makes all people behave badly.	☐	☐
12. Doctors will tell you that smoking is bad for your health.	☐	☐
13. Cigarettes are a waste of money.	☐	☐
14. Smoking can make your teeth yellow.	☐	☐
15. You should never ever take risks.	☐	☐

✔

2.1 Tell the Truth (2)

	True	False
16. Taking a risk is sometimes necessary.	☐	☐
17. Skateboarders should wear protective clothing.	☐	☐
18. If possible you should always cross a road at a pedestrian crossing point.	☐	☐
19. It is not always necessary for everyone to wear a seat belt in a car.	☐	☐
20. It is not necessary to wear a seat belt when travelling by bus or coach because they are so safe.	☐	☐
21. Using candles at home is always dangerous.	☐	☐
22. It is not necessary for all medicines to be locked away.	☐	☐
23. Fireworks should be sold to anyone who wants them.	☐	☐
24. False alarm calls to the emergency services put lives at risk.	☐	☐
25. Broken glass should be disposed of safely.	☐	☐
26. All wild mushrooms are safe to eat.	☐	☐
27. The law states you must wear a helmet whilst cycling.	☐	☐
28. Trying illegal drugs just once is OK.	☐	☐
29. You should never ever give other people your medicines.	☐	☐
30. You are the person most responsible for your safety.	☐	☐

2.1 Tell the Truth (3)

Questions to think about

31. How could just dropping a lighted cigarette start a major fire?

32. How can smoking cannabis affect your health?

33. Why is it dangerous to inject illegal drugs?

34. How can smoke alarms save lives?

35. Why shouldn't you use other people's medicines?

Exercise 3

Scenarios I

Suggested age: 8–9 • Suggested time: 30–40 minutes (this can be extended to two sessions according to the ability of the group)

Outline

An exercise to encourage participants to look at the dangers present in a number of different situations and to consider the options available to the people involved.

Purpose and expected outcome

- To enable participants to explore possible ways of avoiding dangerous situations.

- To encourage participants to examine the sources of help that are available to those experiencing difficulties.

- To encourage individual responsibility over decisions involving risk taking.

- To challenge attitudes to anti-social or criminal activities, and alcohol or drug use.

- To reinforce safety and healthy living messages.

Method

The teacher or group leader should briefly outline the exercise and split the participants into small groups. Each group should be issued with a copy of one of the scenarios. They should then be asked to discuss the scenario and to answer the following questions:

1. How could the person/persons in the scenario have avoided getting into the particular situation?

2. Where could they get help or advice?

3. What are the possible further problems that they might face if the situation does not change?

4.   Now they are in the situation, what can they do to change it?

The teacher or group leader should allow sufficient time for the group to consider all of the possibilities in the situation, and then ask them to report back to the rest of the class the various points that they have discussed, and the solutions that they have come up with. The rest of the class can comment upon the points raised and the suggested solutions.

Notes for teacher or group leader

The session leader will need to be aware that some of the participants may be in personal circumstances that are closely similar to those in the scenarios, and will need to be sensitive to this. It may be advisable to remove a particular scenario if this is felt to be too 'close to home' for any member of the group.

This exercise can be used as an individual exercise with pupils being asked to consider and answer one or a number of scenarios, verbally or in writing. As an alternative the teacher can read one of the scenarios to the class and then hold a general discussion on the points that it raises, and take suggested answers from the class to the questions posed earlier.

A list of agencies that might be able to offer help and advice is given in the Useful Organizations and Websites section of this book.

Follow-up exercises

- Pupils can be asked to research and draw up a list of national or local helping agencies that offer advice in these types of situations.

- Pupils can be asked to collect newspaper reports of real-life situations that are similar to those depicted in the scenarios and to discuss them in the same way as they have discussed the scenarios.

3.1 Alex

Alex is nine and is small for his age. He gets picked on by older boys on his way to school in the morning. They push him around, make fun of his size and force him to give them money. He lives with his mother and older brother and has not seen his father for some years. He has become afraid to walk to school in the morning and has begun to skip school. When he does so he passes the day in a local park where he has become friendly with a group of older men who spend their time drinking.

3.2 Jacob

Jacob is nine years old and lives with his younger brother Ben, who is seven, and his father, who has lost his job. Jacob's dad drinks a lot of beer during the day and is often asleep when Jacob and his brother get home from school. Jacob often cooks evening meals for himself and his brother.

3.3 Zara

Zara is eight and lives at home with her two brothers and her mother. Her elder brother is 14 and often smokes cannabis at home when his mother is out. He steals things from the local shops to sell at school to raise the money to buy his cannabis. Zara loves her brother and has read that smoking cannabis could make him very ill. She tried telling her brother to stop using cannabis and he got very angry and told her to mind her own business.

3.4 Tablets

Two nine-year-old boys have been taken to hospital from school, as they both became very ill during the lunch break. Nobody seems to know why, but they were seen buying some tablets from an older boy outside of the school. This boy told them that the tablets would make them feel really good.

3.5 Hannah

Hannah is eight and walks to school on her own. She likes to get there early so that she can play with her friends before lessons begin. One day she comes across three older boys from another school who are sitting on a seat by the path smoking cigarettes. One of them lives near Hannah and knows her name. He calls her over and offers her a cigarette. Hannah is tempted and accepts the cigarette. The boy lights it for her and she begins to smoke. It makes her cough and feel sick and the boys laugh at her. The next day the boys are there again and again offer her a cigarette. Not wanting to look foolish she accepts it and this time smokes all of it. Hannah stops each day that week for a cigarette and the boys tell her to bring some of her own next time. She does not have enough money to buy them and so she steals some money from home for them. Meeting her new friends soon becomes something that Hannah looks forward to everyday.

3.6 Jon and Billy

Jon is nine and is very friendly with Billy who is the same age as him and lives in the next street. The two boys have played together for several years and their mothers are also friends with each other. During one summer Jon begins to notice that Billy will not talk about what he does when he isn't with Jon. Billy also seems to be very short-tempered and grumpy. Jon discovers that Billy has been sniffing lighter fuel gas in the woods behind his house with some older boys.

Exercise 4

Do the Right Thing I

Suggested age: 8–9 • Suggested time: 40 minutes

Outline

An exercise consisting of a storyline within which are embedded eight different incidents, which require the reader or readers to consider a number of courses of action that could be taken by the characters in the story.

Purpose and expected outcome

- To demonstrate that personal experiences of health and safety situations are commonplace in everyday life.

- To enable participants to consider and explore the implications of a range of varying actions in situations where the health and safety of the individual and others is potentially at risk.

- To reinforce safety and healthy living messages.

Method

The exercise worksheet outlines a story of 'everyday life' in which the characters come across eight separate incidents together with a number of suggested courses of action for each. Participants, whether working singly, in pairs or in small groups, should read through the story, and as they encounter each incident then pause to consider the alternative courses of action provided, or suggest a course of action of their own. As another option, the teacher or group leader could read out the story to the participants, pausing at the relevant points.

The teacher or group leader should decide whether participants are asked to report their chosen action on each individual incident as they are encountered, or report back on all eight incidents after completion of the worksheet. Where participants are working in groups, consideration can be given to appointing a spokesperson for each group.

All participants in this exercise should be given the necessary time and resources to consider their chosen actions and if necessary write them down.

Teachers or group leaders should ask participants to give reasons why they have chosen or rejected different courses of action. Other participants should be encouraged to comment on the chosen courses of action and suggest alternatives if time allows.

Notes for teacher or group leader

Teachers and group leaders should be sensitive to the possibility that some participants may be adversely affected by some incidents within the story due to personal experience.

The following guidance notes pertaining to each situation and the alternative courses of action provided are not intended to be comprehensive and exhaustive. Many of the positive and negative aspects of any of the courses of action will be self-evident, and may arise out of group discussions. The notes are intended as guidance only.

It is worth noting that in many instances a suggested course of action will involve passing information about the actions of others to a responsible adult. This is likely to raise the difficult issue of informing or 'grassing'. Participants may object that they do not want to get their friends 'in trouble' but need to consider that a lack of such action may lead to greater risk and harm to their friends, and others.

Suggested answers

(A) Finding an abandoned mini motor bike
Choices:

1. Start it up and take it in turns to ride it.
   Very dangerous – with no helmet or suitable clothing, and possibly no experience or training, accident is likely. You have no knowledge of how safe the bike is. Legal risks as the bike may have been stolen, and by taking it and riding it you could be seen as stealing it.

2. Tell the police about it.
   Good move – bike may be stolen. Police will arrange removal to safe place.

3. Wheel it home and put it in the shed.
   Possible move if police are then informed straight away – otherwise it could be considered theft.

4. Authors' suggestion.
   2 above – or inform a responsible adult.

(B) Seeing some boys trying to set fire to a building
Choices:

1. Stand and watch.
   Achieves nothing and may be dangerous. You may be blamed for fire.

2. Warn the boys that you will tell the police if they light the fire.
Possible move but other group may become aggressive.

3. Call the fire brigade on your mobile phone.
Good move – remember to give exact location.

4. Authors' suggestion.
Warn boys not to do it – if ignored then call police and/or fire brigade. Remain near scene to give witness information to police.

(C) Wading across to the island
Choices:

1. Use the same route that was used the year before.
Risky – water will be deeper following the rain.

2. Get the tallest person to go first.
Risky for them – water may be too deep – what will you do if they get into difficulties?

3. Use a long stick to feel how deep the water is in front of you.
Risky – stick may sink into the mud, become stuck, or break.

4. Authors' suggestion.
Wading seems very risky with water being deeper following rain. Better to wait until water level returns to normal.

(D) Seeing a man beating his dog
Choices:

1. Do nothing – it's the man's dog and his business.
This achieves nothing.

2. Shout at the man to leave the dog alone.
Possible move – may anger man, but may also bring him to his senses.

3. Ask the man to stop hurting the dog.
Good move – man may have lost his temper with the dog over something and you may bring him to his senses.

4. Authors' suggestion.
3 above. Remember description of man and dog and give them to responsible adult on return home. If beating severe consider calling police on mobile phone.

(E) A boy offers a cannabis cigarette
Choices:

1. Just say no.
Good plan – keeps you safe but boy will still offer it to others.

2. Buy the drug and smoke it.

Cannabis is an illegal drug and potentially very harmful to health, particularly that of young people.

3. Call the police on your mobile phone.
    Good move – be careful not to let boy know what you are doing as he may become aggressive.

4. Authors' suggestion.
    3 above, or tell a responsible person.

(F) Finding a hole in the railway fence
Choices:

1. Try and close up the hole by pulling the wire fencing back.
    Good plan – but remember to tell a responsible adult about the hole to prevent danger to others.

2. Squeeze through the hole and take great care crossing the train tracks.
    Very dangerous – trains travel at very high speeds and you may not make it across – also many train tracks have electrified third rail which can kill instantly if touched.

3. Walk on and ignore the hole, and go over the footbridge.
    Keeps you safe, but if hole is left unrepaired then others are at risk.

4. Authors' suggestion.
    1 above.

(G) Seeing someone about to climb up a pole to free a kite
Choices:

1. Suggest that they use a long stick.
    Risky – unless stick is very dry it may conduct electricity and give a dangerous shock.

2. Stand and watch.
    Achieves nothing and does not promote safety.

3. Help by allowing one of the others to stand on your shoulders.
    Very dangerous. You are helping someone else to take a dangerous risk. If they touch electric wires then you may also get shocked.

4. Authors' suggestion.
    Wires may not be telephone. They are likely to be carrying electricity, possibly high voltage. Best course of action is to tell the others to leave kite where it is and ask for help from a responsible adult.

(H) Robin being left alone all night
Choices:

1. Tell Robin to be careful.
    Achieves very little – Robin still at considerable risk.

2. Invite her to stay at your house.
   Possible – deals with the problem for tonight but does little in the long term. You will need to get mum's permission.

3. Take her to your house and get an adult to report Robin's mum to the authorities.
   Possible – taking Robin to your house is a good idea, but it may be possible for responsible adult to talk to Robin's mum and resolve situation rather than reporting her to the authorities.

4. Authors' suggestion.
   3 above.

Follow-up exercises

- The situations below could be acted out in role play in group work or presented as the subject of assemblies.

- Participants could be asked to create further realistic scenarios and suggest correct courses of action.

- Participants could be asked to research similar incidents reported in the media and discuss the actions taken by those involved and the outcomes.

- Contact could be made with the various emergency services to provide up-to-date information and advice.

4.1 A Long Day Out

Alexi was an only child and lived at home with his mum and grandmother. His mum went out to work all day and left home around eight every morning. One day during half term Alexi told his grandmother that he was going to meet some of his friends and spend the day playing in the woods at the top of the street where he lived. He asked her if he could have some money to buy lunch from the mobile snack bar that parked near the woods His grandmother told him to be careful, but did not object to his plans.

Alexi collected his football from his room and then met up with three of his friends, Robin, Clayton and Furat. They walked up the path at the rear of the local sports club which led to the woods. As they entered the woods Alexi saw something amongst the bushes about ten yards from the path. He and his friends found that it was a mini motor bike. The keys were in the ignition and the engine was warm. They pulled the bike free and wondered what to do next. **(A)**

They then walked up to the top of Tree Top Hill in the middle of the woods. There was an old workshop near the hill top which in the past had been used by foresters. They had played in the building many times before. When they arrived they found that a group of boys were already there. These boys were about a year or so older than Alexi and his friends, and were trying to set fire to a pile of old leaves and branches against one of the walls of the building. The older boys looked up as they approached. **(B)**

Alexi and his friends ran down the hill to a swampy part of the woods that contained a deep lake that they called the 'black hole'. No one knew how deep the lake was in the middle, but it was quite shallow near to one end. Here there was an island about 20 yards out from the edge. They had waded out to the island the summer before and the water had come up to just above their knees. There had been a lot of rain in the previous couple of weeks and the water now looked a bit deeper. Robin suggested that they wade out again, and began to take her shoes and socks off. **(C)**

By now it was lunch time and the four friends were getting hungry. They walked through the woods towards where the snack bar was. As they got closer to the edge of the woods they heard the sound of a man shouting and a dog barking and yelping in pain. They came around a bend in the path and saw ahead of them a man with a large dog on a lead. He seemed angry at the dog and was shouting at it and hitting it with a long stick. The friends were shocked and wondered what to do. **(D)**

Alexi and his friends reached the snack bar and stood in the queue. They were talking about what they would buy for lunch when a boy, who looked about 16 years old, called them over. He asked them if they wanted to buy a cannabis cigarette. He told them that it was cheap and that they would enjoy smoking it. Clayton said that his mum had told him cannabis was dangerous but the older boy laughed and said that was nonsense. He said that no one ever got hurt by just trying cannabis once. The friends looked at each other. **(E)**

After their lunch they decided to walk to another part of the woods where they knew there was a large open grassy area that was good for playing football. To get there, they had to walk alongside the fence that followed the main railway line, then over a footbridge. On the way they found that part of the fencing had been pulled back to make a hole big enough for someone to squeeze through. Furat said that if they crossed over the railway line here, and found another hole in the fence on the other side, they would save a lot of time. **(F)**

Arriving at the grassy area, they put down their coats to make a goal. It was a windy day and some other boys and girls from their school were flying a kite nearby. Suddenly one of the boys in this group shouted to his friends that his kite was stuck in some wires that ran on wooden poles along the edge of the field. The boy said that he was going to climb up the pole to get his kite. Robin told him it was dangerous, but the boy called her stupid, and said that as they were only telephone wires they were safe. Alexi and his friends didn't know what to do. **(G)**

They finished their game of football and set off for home. Furat started to tell the others what her mum was making for her tea, and Clayton told them that his dad did all the cooking in his house and cooked some great meals. Robin then told the boys that she would have to get her own tea as her mum was staying at her friend's that night, and she would be alone at home until around dinner time the next day. Alexi thought that that wasn't safe and wondered what he should do. **(H)**

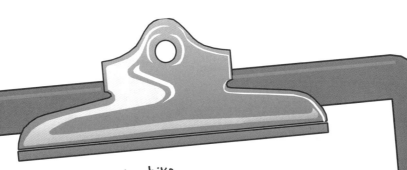

(A) Finding a mini motor bike

Choices:

1. Start it up and take it in turns to ride it.
2. Tell the police about it.
3. Wheel it home and put it in the shed.
4. None of the above – your suggestion.

(B) Seeing some boys trying to set fire to a building

Choices:

1. Stand and watch.
2. Warn the boys that you will tell the police if they light the fire.
3. Call the fire brigade on your mobile phone.
4. None of the above – your suggestion.

(C) Wading across to the island

Choices:

1. Use the same route that was used the year before.
2. Get the tallest person to go first.
3. Use a long stick to feel how deep the water is in front of you.
4. None of the above – your suggestion.

(D) Seeing a man beating his dog

Choices:

1. Do nothing – it's the man's dog and his business.
2. Shout at the man to leave the dog alone.
3. Ask the man to stop hurting the dog.
4. None of the above – your suggestion.

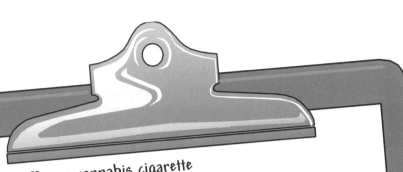

(E) A boy offers a cannabis cigarette

Choices:

1. Just say no.
2. Buy the drug and smoke it.
3. Call the police on your mobile phone.
4. None of the above – your suggestion.

(F) Finding a hole in the railway fence

Choices:

1. Try and close up the hole by pulling the wire fencing back.
2. Squeeze through the hole and take great care crossing the train tracks.
3. Walk on and ignore the hole, and go over the footbridge.
4. None of the above – your suggestion.

(G) Seeing someone about to climb up a pole to free a kite

Choices:

1. Suggest that they use a long stick.
2. Stand and watch.
3. Help by allowing one of the others to stand on your shoulders.
4. None of the above – your suggestion.

(H) Robin being left alone all night

Choices:

1. Tell Robin to be careful.
2. Invite her to stay at your house.
3. Take her to your house and get an adult to report Robin's mum to the authorities (school/social services/police).
4. None of the above – your suggestion.

Exercise 5

Risks Pyramid Ten

Suggested age: 8–9 • Suggested time: 30–40 minutes

Outline

An exercise to encourage participants to assess and classify the potential for danger in a number of activities that present different levels of risk.

Purpose and expected outcome

- To encourage the development of risk assessment strategies.
- To place assessed risks in their order of potential danger.
- To encourage participants to consider risk assessment decisions of others.
- To challenge attitudes to risk taking.
- To reinforce safety and healthy living messages.

Method

The worksheets should be copied and cut up to produce sufficient sets for small group work. If it is intended to use the sets repeatedly they can be laminated. The teacher or group leader should briefly outline the purpose of the exercise, and split the class up into small groups. The first set of cards should be distributed, one identical set to each group. The teacher or group leader may decide, either independently or in consultation with the participants, which of the two sets of cards to use first. Groups should be asked to consider the risk potential of the activity printed on each card and to select ten of them that, in their opinion, present the most potentially dangerous risks. Having selected their ten cards the group should then arrange them in the 'pyramid ten' layout, as shown.

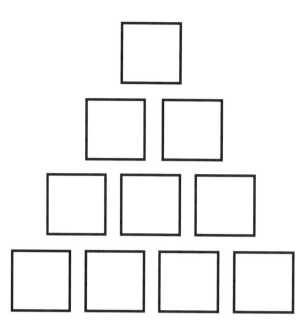

The top position should be occupied by the card that, in the opinion of the group, contains the activity that carries with it the most risk potential. The two positions in the second row should be occupied by the cards that contain the next most potentially dangerous activity, the third row the three next most risky and the bottom row the four judged the least risky.

When sufficient time has elapsed for each group to arrange its cards in a 'pyramid ten', they should report their choices and placings back to the rest of the class. A simple scoring system can be used to arrive at a common 'pyramid ten'. The card placed at the top by any group should be awarded one point, cards placed in the second row two points, the third row three points and those placed in the bottom row should be awarded four points. Cards not selected for inclusion in any group's 'pyramid ten' should be awarded five points. When all of the groups have reported back, the points can be added up to produce a class 'pyramid ten' shape. The card that scores the lowest number of points should be placed at the top, the next two in the second row and so on until the shape is complete. The two cards that have the highest scores are left out. The teacher can then ask each group why they chose to place a particular card where they did. Groups can also be asked to justify leaving out certain cards or placing them in a lower position. General discussion can then take place.

The second set of cards can be used immediately following the first set or on a separate occasion.

Notes for teacher or group leader

There are no totally right or wrong answers in this exercise. It is an opportunity for participants to discuss their views and, having come to an agreement, indicate their reasoning. Providing the group has given sufficient thought to the placings and are prepared to explain their reasoning, then any placing order is valid. When a group is unable to agree a particular placing, then a simple vote may resolve the dispute. When a dispute is not resolved by voting, then a separate minority placing order may be accepted. Every effort, however, should be made to achieve agreement.

Follow-up exercises

- Creating a further set of cards with other risk-taking behaviours.

- Creating a set of cards that contain reasons for young people to become involved in risk-taking behaviour.

5.1 Everyday Risky Behaviour (1)

Not wearing a seat belt in a car	Roller blading
Smoking cigarettes	Drinking alcohol
Climbing trees	Playing football in the road

5.1 Everyday Risky Behaviour (2)

Eating too much chocolate	Not eating enough vegetables and fruit
Sniffing solvents	Playing with matches
Snowboarding	Being out alone after dark

5.2 Everyday Risky Behaviour (1)

Running across the road	Running away from home
Using a sharp knife	Helping yourself to medicine
Using superglue	BMX trick riding

46   Copyright © David Emmett and Graeme Nice 2008

5.2 Everyday Risky Behaviour (2)

Lighting a campfire	Carrying boiling water
Getting a hot dish out of the oven	Ice skating
Climbing a tall ladder	Vandalizing a public telephone

Exercise 6

Warning Signs

Suggested age: 9–10 • Suggested time: 45 minutes

Outline

An exercise comprising images and safety messages depicting everyday objects, substances and situations that can be found in and around the home, school, etc. or that are commonly experienced, designed to increase participants' awareness and understanding of warning and safety information concerning potential risks to themselves or others.

Purpose and expected outcome

- To encourage and increase awareness and understanding of common warning signs and labels.

- To enable participants to discuss potential risks to self and others.

- To increase participants' awareness of potential risky situations where no such warning information is given.

- To reinforce safety and healthy living messages.

Method

The exercise comprises sheet **A** depicting 20 images, lettered A to T, of substances, objects and situations, most of which could be seen daily, whilst others are less usual. Sheet **B** contains images of 24 warning signs or labels. Depending on the time available, the number of participants and their considered ability, sheets A and B can be given out individually, to small groups, pairs, or may be considered by the entire group. The group leader should explain that participants are to decide which warning sign or label shown on sheet B are relevant to which image on sheet A. The group leader will be aware that more than one of the signs and labels on sheet B may be relevant to a particular image shown on sheet A, or to none at all. Once participants have completed their chosen allocation of signs and labels, the teacher or group leader should encourage discussion as to why they feel they are relevant, explaining the potential risks involved. It will be noted that the image of drug abuse (M – needle and syringe, powder and tablets) will in real life have no warning labels or signs attached to it, and thus the potential dangers will have to be calculated by any potential user. On the other hand, the image of cigarettes (I) has not been provided with a relevant warning label on sheet B, but in real life every packet will show such a label, which cigarette smokers appear to take little notice of. Discussion should be encouraged on these two points.

Notes for teacher or group leader

Any situation that participants might find themselves in could present potential risks. Warning signs and labels are a common feature of everyday life but their very commonness lessens their impact. Some situations, however, come with no such warnings attached and the risks may be less obvious, but still need serious consideration. Teachers and group leaders should be sensitive to the possibility that some participants may have had personal experience of one or more of the risky situations included.

This exercise contains some words and expressions that may be unfamiliar to participants and require further explanation. These include the following:

- heavy plant

- solvent use

- irritant

- flammable

- hard hat.

Follow-up exercises

- Participants can be asked to draw up a list of warning signs or labels that they find on products and appliances in and around their own homes. It must be made clear to them that this exercise should only be carried out with the supervision of a parent or other responsible adult.

- Participants can be asked to devise and create new and improved warning signs or labels for the images that come with this exercise or for other substances or situations that are not covered by this exercise.

Sheet A

Sheet B

1 PEDESTRIANS CROSSING

2 DANGER! Heavy Plant Turning

3 Avoid contact with skin and eyes

4 KEEP OUT OF REACH OF CHILDREN

5 POISON

6 SOLVENT Use can kill instantly

7 WARNING! May contain nuts

8 WASH HANDS AFTER USE

9 DANGER OF DEATH KEEP OFF

10 Do not cross WAIT!

11 HARD HAT AREA No admission without proper headwear

12 IRRITANT

13 DANGER! DEEP WATER

14 CAUTION WET FLOOR

15 FLAMMABLE

16 WARNING! Do not burn even when empty

17 FASTEN SEATBELTS

18 NO SMOKING Switch off engine!

19 Stop when lights flash

20 Do not exceed the stated dose

21 FIRE EXIT DO NOT OBSTRUCT

22 USE BY 16 FEB 2007

23 BEWARE OF THE DOG

24 FALLING ROCKS

Exercise 7

Get the Facts

Suggested age: 9–10 • Suggested time: 40 minutes

Outline

A quiz in 'true or false' and short answer format, designed to allow participants to check out their knowledge and understanding of substance misuse and other risky behaviours.

This quiz is the second of four such quizzes, one for each age group, contained in this volume. A number of similar questions are to be found in some of the quizzes. This is deliberate and allows for the answers given by participants to become more comprehensive as their maturity and understanding develops.

Purpose and expected outcome

- To provide accurate information about drugs and drug use, alcohol use, smoking and other risky behaviour.

- To encourage thoughtful debate about such issues.

- To encourage good decision making.

- To reinforce safety and healthy living messages.

Method

The quiz consists of 45 questions designed to be suitable for young people aged nine to ten. The first three sheets contain a total of 40 questions, which all require answers of either 'true' or 'false'. The fourth sheet has five questions which require short paragraph-length answers. The teacher or group leader can decide on the length of the quiz to suit the participants and the time available.

It should be explained to the participants that the purpose of the quiz is not to examine their level of knowledge about such topics as drugs, alcohol, smoking and other forms of risky behaviour but rather to encourage them to consider such issues and check out the

accuracy or otherwise of any knowledge they may already have, and to add useful, accurate and balanced information.

The quiz sheets should be copied and handed out to the participants, and time allowed for them to answer the questions. The teacher or group leader should then go through the answers with the participants using the guidance notes below. Many of the questions will prompt discussion of the question itself and a number of associated issues. This is intended, and should be encouraged.

Participants should be asked to correct their sheets in line with the given answers and keep them for future reference.

Notes for teacher or group leader

Teachers and group leaders should be sensitive to the possibility that some participants may be adversely affected by some statements within this exercise, due to personal experience.

This exercise contains some words and expressions that may be unfamiliar to participants and require further explanation. These include the following:

- prescribed

- addiction

- addicted

- sniffing solvents

- nicotine

- justified

- essential.

Suggested answers

1. **False**. Whilst many drugs can be very harmful to your health, e.g. heroin, nicotine, cannabis, etc., drugs prescribed by a doctor can be very good for your health. However, it should be remembered that even drugs prescribed by the doctor can be harmful if misused.

2. **False**. As 1 above. Also it is sometimes possible for a patient to have an adverse reaction to a prescribed drug that they used in accordance with the doctor's instructions.

3. **True**. Many drugs, including most of the illegal 'street' drugs, some legal drugs, and even some medicinal drugs, can lead to the user becoming addicted or dependent on them. This dependence means that the craving for the drug can be very strong and abstaining from use of the drug can be very difficult.

4. **True**. When used by adults in sensible moderate amounts it will cause few risks to health or safety.

5. **False**. In the UK it is illegal to give alcohol to those under five years of age except for medical reasons. It is therefore legal for those over five to drink alcohol at home. However, if parents allowed excessive use it could be considered a form of neglect or abuse in the eyes of the law.

6. **True**. Excessive alcohol use can lead to increased blood pressure and serious heart disease.

7. **False**. Nicotine is a highly addictive drug. Few, if any, tobacco smokers escape without becoming addicted to this drug. It can be very difficult for some people to give up smoking once addicted.

8. **True**. Nicotine, carbon monoxide and other harmful chemicals from the burning tobacco travel in the mother's bloodstream and can reach the foetus. This can result in impaired development and reduced birth weight. Tobacco smoke can also be harmful to young children and babies (sudden infant death syndrome).

9. **False**. They just look foolish and sad, even if they feel more grown up.

10. **True**. Sniffing solvents is *highly dangerous*. There is a danger of sudden death caused by overstimulation of the heart or asphyxiation caused by swelling of the throat tissues or inhalation of vomit. Users also expose themselves to a high level of risk of accidents whilst intoxicated.

11. **True**. As 10 above.

12. **False**. Cannabis can lead to changes in the user's mood, which can only be achieved through changes within the brain. Smoking cannabis can lead to loss of short-term memory, impaired judgement, dry mouth, lethargy, decreased blood pressure, bloodshot eyes, dizziness, confusion, anxiety, panic, paranoia, psychosis, depression, schizophrenia, and has a potential to cause cancers and breathing disorders. For many people the decision to start smoking cannabis is followed by the decision to use other, more dangerous, drugs.

13. **True**. In the UK in the early 1980s equal proportions of boys and girls between 11 and 15 years of age smoked regularly. In 2004, 10 per cent of girls between 11 and 15 years of age were regular smokers, compared with 7 per cent of boys. Government statistics released in February 2006 in the USA indicated that the percentage of teenage girls who were regular smokers surpassed that of boys.

14. **True**. In the UK it is an offence to be intoxicated in a public place.

15. **True**. Many addicted drug users spend large sums of money on their drugs of choice. For many such users this money is raised by theft, drug dealing or prostitution.

16. **False**. Many illegal drugs are very impure, containing many contaminating substances. These substances may not dissolve completely and lead to blockages of blood vessels. Injecting drugs carries the risk of vein collapse and of infections such as HIV/AIDS and hepatitis if needles and syringes are shared. Once a drug is injected it can not be easily removed from the body, thus any adverse reactions are potentially more dangerous.

17. **False**. Tea, coffee and cola all contain caffeine, a mild stimulant drug. In small quantities it provides a refreshing increase in energy levels; in larger quantities it can lead to headaches, anxiety, agitation, tremors and insomnia. Excessive use can lead to development of addiction and, in very extreme cases, death has been known.

18. **True**. The breath, hair and clothing of smokers often smell very stale and unpleasant. Even being in the same room as someone who is smoking can make your hair and clothing smell in the same way.

19. **True**. Excessive consumption of alcohol does lead some people to behave in an unthinking, careless, noisy or aggressive way.

20. **True**. They may not be suitable for you and may lead to an adverse reaction.

21. **True**. Even clean and unused needles and syringes can be dangerous in the wrong hands. A used needle and syringe can be especially dangerous as it may contain blood, bacteria, drugs or viruses.

22. **False**. In January 2007 the UK government announced its intention to raise the minimum age at which a person may legally purchase tobacco or tobacco related products from 16 to 18 years. This change is scheduled to take effect in October 2007. In the USA the minimum age at which cigarettes may be purchased is 18 years.

23. **True**. A drug habit can cost many hundreds of pounds each week. The authors of this book have known many drug users with habits costing over £1000 per week.

24. **False**. Cider contains between 5 and 10 per cent alcohol by volume. This makes it just as strong as beer, or stronger, with the same potential to make a person very drunk.

25. **True**. Misuse of all three can become extremely expensive (see answer 23). It is difficult to consider use of street drugs or cigarettes as anything other than an expensive waste of money. However, sensible and moderate use of alcohol may give some value for money in the form of relaxation and pleasure.

26. **True**. The use of alcohol and many street drugs can lead to a slowing of brain activity and a lowering of the ability to concentrate.

27. **True**. The tar in tobacco is deposited on the smoker's teeth and fingers, giving them a brownish yellow colour.

28. **False**. Risk taking is a natural part of most young people's personality. Taking risks can be exciting and enjoyable and can enhance personal development. The important thing is to know the exact nature of the risk you are taking and what the possible drawbacks and benefits are. Also, circumstances may arise when it is necessary to take a risk to achieve something important such as saving someone's life.

29. **False**. In the UK you are not required to wear a helmet whilst cycling. However, should you fall or be knocked off your bike, wearing a helmet could save you from a potentially life-threatening head injury.

30. **True**. There is no legal requirement to wear protective clothing whilst skateboarding. However, skateboarding is a potentially risky sport and it is that risk that makes it so exciting. The level of risk to the skateboarder can be reduced by wearing a helmet and knee and elbow pads without making it less exciting.

31. **False**. In the UK children under the age of 12 years, or below 135 cm in height, must be seated in an appropriate seat and wear an appropriate seat harness. A child over three years of age may travel unrestrained in the back of a car in which rear seat belts are not required to be fitted. In the USA, age limits for seat belt use vary between states.

32. **False**. In the UK trains are not currently fitted with seat belts. However, deaths and injuries occur due to passengers being thrown from their seats during train accidents. On the other hand, all passenger planes have seat belts fitted that must be worn during take off and landing and during periods of turbulence.

33. **True**. A small fire can quickly escalate into a big one.

34. **True**. Most medicines, if used incorrectly, have the potential to cause harm. This is particularly so when incorrectly used by young people. They should be kept safely out of reach of young people at all times, and only given when necessary by a responsible adult.

35. **False**. This could lead to an explosion and cause serious injury or death.

36. **False**. An element of risk can make a sport very exciting. However, it is necessary to understand the nature of that risk and take action to control it, e.g. wearing protective clothing.

37. **False**. This could lead to an explosion and cause serious injury.

38. **True**. Whilst many wild mushrooms are both safe and delicious to eat, there are many highly poisonous varieties. Some of these poisonous varieties look very similar to edible ones. Care needs to be taken to collect only the safe varieties.

39. **True**. See answer 28.

40. **True**. Smoke alarms will sound long before the levels of smoke become dangerously high. This provides people with valuable time to evacuate a burning

building. Many fires start at night when the occupants of a building are asleep. Smoke alarms will wake such occupants and allow them to escape.

Questions to think about

41. Whilst the emergency services are wasting time on a false call they can not be so readily available to help someone who is genuinely in need of help. Minutes, even seconds, count when someone is in serious need of help. False alarm calls divert these resources.

42. Parents, those caring for you, doctor, nurse.

43. Smoking cigarettes causes damage to the lungs that makes them less efficient, and thus less able to pass oxygen into the bloodstream to power the muscles. Carbon monoxide gas in tobacco smoke takes the place of oxygen being carried in a smoker's blood and provides no nourishment to muscles.

44. To name but a few:

   - physical health problems
   - mental health problems
   - legal problems
   - addiction
   - street drug impurity
   - injecting
   - education and employment difficulties.

45. For reasons that are not yet fully understood, some people seem to develop addictions to street drugs, cigarettes or alcohol more easily than others. There is some evidence that some of this predisposition may be genetically inherited. For instance, the offspring of alcoholics are more likely to become alcoholics themselves, even when not exposed to the social influence of their alcoholic parents.

Follow-up exercises

- The quiz will have raised many issues connected with risky behaviour. Any of these can be followed up with discussions, role-play exercises, story writing, or researching local and national newspapers and magazines.

✔

7.1 Get the Facts (1)

	True	False
1. All drugs can be bad for your health.	☐	☐
2. Prescribed drugs are always safe.	☐	☐
3. Using drugs can lead to addiction.	☐	☐
4. Alcohol can be used safely.	☐	☐
5. It is illegal to drink alcohol at home if you are under 12.	☐	☐
6. Alcohol can be bad for your heart.	☐	☐
7. Nicotine is not really addictive.	☐	☐
8. Cigarette smoke is harmful to babies.	☐	☐
9. Young people who smoke look more grown up.	☐	☐
10. Sniffing solvents can make you very sick.	☐	☐
11. Sniffing solvents can kill you first time.	☐	☐
12. Using cannabis doesn't affect the brain.	☐	☐
13. More girls than boys smoke.	☐	☐
14. Getting drunk in public is illegal.	☐	☐
15. Many drug users commit crime.	☐	☐

7.1 Get the Facts (2)

	True	False
16. Injecting drugs is the safest way to use them.	☐	☐
17. You cannot become addicted to the legal drug contained in tea, coffee and cola.	☐	☐
18. Smoking cigarettes can make your breath and clothes smell.	☐	☐
19. Drinking alcohol makes some people behave carelessly.	☐	☐
20. You should never use other people's medicines.	☐	☐
21. Needles and syringes are always dangerous.	☐	☐
22. Young people are allowed to buy cigarettes for an adult.	☐	☐
23. Drug habits can be very costly.	☐	☐
24. Cider will not make you very drunk.	☐	☐
25. Drugs, cigarettes and alcohol are simply a waste of money.	☐	☐
26. Using alcohol or drugs can affect your concentration at school.	☐	☐
27. Smoking can stain your teeth and fingers.	☐	☐
28. Taking a risk is never justified.	☐	☐
29. By law, you must wear a helmet whilst cycling.	☐	☐
30. Skateboarders do not need to wear protective clothing.	☐	☐

7.1 Get the Facts (3)

	True	False
31. Small children in cars do not need to wear a seat belt.	☐	☐
32. Trains are so safe that seat belts are not needed.	☐	☐
33. You should never leave a lighted candle or fire unattended.	☐	☐
34. All medicines at home should be locked away safely.	☐	☐
35. It is OK to light a barbecue with petrol/gasoline.	☐	☐
36. Sports such as boxing or motor racing are dangerous and should be banned.	☐	☐
37. It's safe to dispose of an empty aerosol can on a bonfire.	☐	☐
38. Some mushrooms are poisonous.	☐	☐
39. Some people take risks to make life more interesting.	☐	☐
40. Smoke alarms in houses are essential.	☐	☐

7.1 Get the Facts (4)

41. Making a false alarm call to the emergency services is dangerous and illegal. What might happen if someone did this?

42. List those people who it would be safe to accept medicines from.

43. Why will smoking cigarettes make you less fit for sport?

44. List the reasons why people shouldn't take illegal drugs.

45. Trying drugs just once can be very dangerous. Why is this so?

Exercise 8

Scenarios 2

Suggested age: 9–10 • Suggested time: 30 minutes

Outline

An exercise to encourage participants to look at the dangers present in a number of different situations and to consider the options available to the people involved.

Purpose and expected outcome

- To enable participants to explore possible ways of avoiding dangerous situations.

- To encourage participants to examine the sources of help that are available to those experiencing difficulties.

- To encourage individual responsibility over decisions involving risk taking.

- To challenge attitudes to anti-social or criminal activities, and drink or drug use.

- To reinforce safety and healthy living messages.

Method

The teacher or group leader should briefly outline the exercise and split the participants into small groups. Each group should be issued with a copy of one of the scenarios. They should then be asked to discuss the scenario and to answer the following questions.

1. How could the person/persons in the scenario have avoided getting into the particular situation?

2. Where could they get help or advice?

3. What are the possible further problems that they might face if the situation does not change?

4. Now they are in the situation, what can they do to change it?

As an alternative the teacher or group leader could read out the scenarios to the participants.

The teacher or group leader should allow sufficient time for the group to consider all of the possibilities in the situation, and then ask them to report back to the rest of the class the various points that they have discussed, and the solutions that they have come up with. The rest of the class can comment upon the points raised and the suggested solutions.

Notes for teacher or group leader

The session leader will need to be aware that some of the participants may be in personal circumstances that are closely similar to those in the scenarios, and will need to be sensitive to this. It may be advisable to remove a particular scenario if this is felt to be too 'close to home' for any member of the group.

This exercise can be used as an individual exercise with pupils being asked to consider and answer one or a number of scenarios, verbally or in writing. As an alternative the teacher can read one of the scenarios to the class and then hold a general discussion on the points that it raises, and take suggested answers from the class to the questions posed earlier.

A list of agencies that might be able to offer help and advice is given in the Useful Organizations and Websites section of this book.

Follow-up exercises

- Pupils can be asked to research and draw up a list of national or local helping agencies that offer advice in these types of situations.

- Pupils can be asked to collect newspaper reports of real-life situations that are similar to those depicted in the scenarios and to discuss them in the same way as they have discussed the scenarios.

8.1 Aziz and Will

Aziz is ten years old. His family have recently moved to a new town after his father changed jobs. He has not found it easy to make friends at his new school but has become friendly with Will, a boy in his class. Both of Aziz's parents go to work and do not return home until after 5.30 in the evening. Will has started to come to Aziz's home after school to watch television and play computer games. One afternoon Will opens a cupboard in the living room at Aziz's home and takes out a bottle of wine. He suggests that he and Aziz try some. Both boys drink a mouthful each. The next afternoon Will suggests that they both drink some more wine.

8.2 Amital

Amital is ten years old and lives with his parents and three older sisters. He finds life at home and at school boring and has few friends of his own age. He has recently made friends with a group of teenage boys and girls who spend time sitting around under a bridge over the local canal. The teenagers regularly get drunk and many of them smoke cannabis. Amital finds it exciting to spend time with them and has started to join in their drinking and cannabis smoking.

8.3 Georgia

Georgia is nine and lives with her aunt. Her parents split up two years ago. Her aunt is kind to her but Georgia is very unhappy and misses her parents very much. She has begun to sniff lighter fuel gas in her room every evening to help her forget her worries and cope with her unhappy feelings.

8.4 Kevin and Rash

Kevin is nine and often gets into trouble at school. He is noisy in class and does not always do what the teacher tells him to. He is popular with many of the other pupils, who think he is funny. During break time he is usually the leader of a group of boys and girls who play football in the playground. These football games are often very rough and other children sometimes get knocked over. Rash is in the same class as Kevin and has tried talking to him about the roughness of the football games. Kevin just laughed at Rash. One day, during one of these football games, one of Rash's friends is knocked over and badly grazes her arm.

8.5 Jason

Jason is ten and is regularly picked up from school by his father in his car. Jason notices that his father often smells of alcohol when he picks him up and sometimes he seems not to drive very well at all.

8.6 Clayton

Clayton is nine and is bullied at school by a group of older boys and girls. He has tried keeping away from them in the playground during break but they seem to find him wherever he is. They sometimes take his dinner money and once they took his phone from him and used it before giving it back. He has told his parents about it but they have told him that he just needs to stand up for himself.

Exercise 9

Do the Right Thing 2

Suggested age: 9–10 • Suggested time: 40 minutes

Outline

An exercise consisting of a storyline within which are embedded eight different incidents, which require the reader or readers to consider a number of courses of action that could be taken by the characters in the story.

Purpose and expected outcome

- To demonstrate that personal experiences of health and safety situations are commonplace in everyday life.

- To enable participants to consider and explore the implications of a range of varying actions in situations where the health and safety of the individual and others is potentially at risk.

- To reinforce safety and healthy living messages.

Method

The exercise worksheet outlines a story of 'everyday life' in which the characters come across eight separate incidents together with a number of suggested courses of action for each. Participants, whether working singly, in pairs or in small groups, should read through the story, and as they encounter each incident then pause to consider the alternative courses of action provided, or suggest a course of action of their own. As another option, the teacher or group leader could read out the story to the participants, pausing at the relevant points.

The teacher or group leader should decide whether participants are asked to report their chosen action on each individual incident as they are encountered, or report back on all eight incidents after completion of the story. Where participants are working in groups, consideration can be given to appointing a spokesperson for each group.

All participants in this exercise should be given the necessary time and resources to consider their chosen actions and if necessary write them down.

Teachers or group leaders should ask participants to give reasons why they have chosen or rejected different courses of action. Other participants should be encouraged to comment on the chosen courses of action and suggest alternatives if time allows.

Notes for teacher or group leader

Teachers and group leaders should be sensitive to the possibility that some participants may be adversely affected by some incidents within the story due to personal experience.

The following guidance notes pertaining to each situation and the alternative courses of action provided are not intended to be comprehensive and exhaustive. Many of the positive and negative aspects of any of the courses of action will be self-evident, and may arise out of group discussions. The notes are intended as guidance only.

It is worth noting that in many instances a suggested course of action will involve passing information about the actions of others to a responsible adult. This is likely to raise the difficult issue of informing or 'grassing'. Participants may object that they do not want to get their friends 'in trouble' but need to consider that a lack of such action may lead to greater risk and harm to their friends, and others.

Suggested answers

(A) Offered a lift by a boy thought to use drink and drugs
Choices:

1. Decide to accept the lift and see what happens.
    Very risky – boy may be driving under influence of drugs or drink.

2. Ignore the boy.
    Possible – but the boy may persist and get angry if you carry on ignoring him.

3. Say thanks but refuse the lift.
    Good plan – he may persist and you will need to be firm but polite.

4. Authors' suggestion.
    3 above. Good idea to tell mother or other responsible adult on return home.

(B) Offered a cigarette by a friend
Choices:

1. Accept the cigarette.
    Bad idea. Smoking very harmful to health and may lead to you becoming addicted. Sets bad example to your friends and gives Kirsty the message that smoking is OK.

2. Just say 'No thanks'.
    Possible – keeps you safe and supports Josh and Sam but does nothing to deter Kirsty from smoking.

3. Tell Kirsty she shouldn't be smoking and to put her cigarette out.
    May be effective – depends on your relationship with Kirsty – remember the power of peer pressure.

4. Authors' suggestion.
    Turn down offer and voice your concern and disapproval at Kirsty smoking. Remember the power of peer pressure. The disapproval of her friends may deter Kirsty from smoking.

(C) Upset by Sam's dangerous driving
Choices:

1. Tell Sam he is an idiot and storm off.
    Possible – may show Sam how foolish his behaviour was.

2. Say nothing.
    This achieves nothing and may suggest to Sam that his behaviour was acceptable.

3. Talk to Sam about how upset you are.
    Good plan – if he is truly your friend it will have an effect. Remember the power of peer approval/disapproval.

4. Authors' suggestion.
    3 above. If this does not work then be careful about taking part with Sam in anything that carries risks.

(D) Recognizing a bag snatcher
Choices:

1. Do nothing – it's none of your business.
    This achieves nothing – you, or someone you know, may be the victim next time.

2. Call the police on your mobile phone.
    Good plan – if he is arrested straight away it may save other victims that day.

3. Wait until you get home and tell your mum.
    Possible – but wastes time which allows for more victims. If concerned about calling police then phone home for advice.

4. Authors' suggestion.
    2 or 3 above. Remember that if we say nothing then the thief can simply go on to commit more crimes.

(E) Find some small plastic bags of powder
Choices:

1. Taste the powder to see what it is.
   Very dangerous – may be dangerous drug, or even poison.

2. Put the plastic bag back in the hole in the tree.
   This achieves nothing and may lead to someone else finding it and harming themselves or others.

3. Take the bag to the police station.
   Possible – need to take great care not to become contaminated with the powder.

4. Authors' suggestion.
   Leave the bag where it is and contact police on mobile phone or other nearby phone. May wish to phone home for advice.

(F) Some boys offer you some alcohol
Choices:

1. Accept just a little of it, just to try.
   Risky – you only have their word it is alcohol. If you say yes to a little they may persist and make you drink more. You may like it and drink too much.

2. Invite the boys to sit down with you and share their drink.
   Very dangerous – could lead to you getting drunk with possible dangerous results.

3. Say 'No thanks'.
   Good plan – if they persist, you will need to be polite but firm.

4. Authors' suggestion.
   3 above. It may be necessary for you to get up and walk off – rejoining fairground crowds as soon as possible. If boys become too persistent then seek help from nearest adult that you judge is trustworthy.

(G) See some boys assaulting an old man
Choices:

1. Shout to them to leave the man alone.
   Good plan, but be aware that they may turn on you.

2. Stand and watch.
   This achieves nothing and only shows that you do not care about others.

3. Call the police on your mobile phone.
   Good plan if action 1 fails.

4. Authors' suggestion.
   1 and 3. Remember that even if they leave this old man alone after you shout then they may, in their drunken state, go on to hurt others.

(H) Find a little girl who has been left by her brother
Choices:

  1. Tell the girl to keep waiting.
     Not a good idea. Her brother may not come back, and girl may become more distressed.

  2. Take the girl over to the nearest adult.
     Possible plan, but you need to be satisfied that the adult is trustworthy.

  3. Ring home on your mobile phone and ask for advice.
     Very good plan – if no one answers then consider ringing police.

  4. Authors' suggestion.
     3 above.

Follow-up exercises

- The situations below could be acted out in role play in group work or presented as the subject of assemblies.

- Participants could be asked to create further realistic scenarios and suggest correct courses of action.

- Participants could be asked to research similar incidents reported in the media and discuss the actions taken by those involved and the outcomes.

- Contact could be made with the various emergency services to provide up-to-date information and advice.

9.1 A Day at the Fair

Siobhan had been asking her mother all week to allow her to go with her friends to the fair. This was a travelling fair that had set up on the park near the centre of town. It only came to town once a year, and Siobhan thought that this year she was old enough to be allowed to go with her friends and without any adults. Finally her mother gave in and said that she could as long as she was very careful and came home before dark. She told Siobhan to take her mobile phone with her and to ring home at least twice during the day to let her mum know she was OK.

Saturday morning came and Siobhan left at 10am to meet her friends. Her mother had given her some extra money to spend at the fair. Siobhan was excited as she waited at the bus stop just down the road from her house. She had arranged to meet up with her friends near the entrance to the park and couldn't wait for the bus to arrive. Suddenly a car stopped opposite her and she saw that the driver was a boy she knew of around 18 years old who lived in the same street as her. Siobhan's mother had told her not to have anything to do with this boy as she had heard he was using drugs and alcohol. The boy shouted to her, 'Going to town? Want a lift?' Siobhan didn't know what to do. **(A)**

Siobhan reached the entrance to the park where her three friends from school, Sam, Kirsty and Josh, were waiting for her. Kirsty was smoking a cigarette. She took out a packet and offered one to Siobhan. Kirsty said, 'Want one of these? These two babies didn't.' **(B)**

The four friends entered the fairground and made their way towards the dodgem cars. All of them liked this ride best and had agreed that they would try it out first. They paid for two cars and Siobhan got in with Sam. Sam got in behind the steering wheel and drove off as fast as he could. He crashed very heavily into Kirsty and Josh's car and then into the side of a car containing two very young children. Siobhan saw one of these children hit her head on the front of the dodgem car and start to cry. She shouted to Sam to slow down but he just laughed and called her a sissy. He said that if people didn't like being hit they shouldn't come on the dodgems. He then started to drive the wrong way around the ride. Suddenly he cut across the middle of the ride and crashed into a car with two more children in, and Siobhan was almost thrown out of the car. She began to feel sick. One of the workers in charge of the ride shouted at Sam to pull into the side and get out as he was driving too dangerously. Saying that he was only having some fun, Sam pulled in to the side and he and Siobhan got out. Siobhan was upset and angry at her friend for behaving as he did and wondered what to do. **(C)**

The next ride they tried was the helter-skelter. The four friends climbed up the stairs to the top and found there was a short queue of people waiting to slide down. Josh was looking over the side of the waiting area and saying how much he could see of the whole fairground. Suddenly he called the others over to join him and pointed to a boy aged about 14 who was running through the crowd towards the edge of the fairground. 'I've just seen him snatch a woman's bag,' Josh said. They could all see that the boy was carrying what looked like a handbag. As they watched he disappeared behind one of the fairground vehicles, then after a few seconds they saw him reappear without the bag. They all realized that they knew him. He was the older brother of one of their school friends. **(D)**

By now it was close to lunch time and the four friends were getting hungry. They queued up at the food stall and all bought a bag of chips and a drink each. They sat under a tree near the edge of the park and began to eat their food. They had just started when Kirsty noticed a plastic bag hidden in a hole at the bottom of the tree. She opened the bag and they could see that it contained a number of small plastic bags of white powder. Kirsty started to open one of the little bags. **(E)**

After the friends had eaten their chips, Kirsty lit another cigarette. She offered them again to the others but none wanted to smoke. Just then a group of four older boys came up and asked Kirsty to give them each a cigarette. The boys were all about 13 years old and were carrying bottles of cider and beer. They offered to swap some of their drink for the cigarettes. One of the boys said, 'Here, you can all have some.' **(F)**

About an hour later, the four friends saw the same group of boys again. They now seemed quite drunk. They were gathered around one of the benches in the park and the friends could see that there was an old man laid along the bench. He had a beard, was wearing a big dirty coat, and looked very scruffy. He appeared to be asleep. The boys were laughing and one of them was pouring liquid from a bottle over the old man. Then they saw one of the boys begin to light matches and throw them onto the sleeping old man. **(G)**

By now it was getting late and time to go home. Siobhan had phoned her mum, as promised, and told her that she would be catching the next bus. As the four friends walked to the entrance to the park they saw a little girl of about six standing by the park gates and crying. They asked her what was wrong and she said that she was lost. She had come to the fair with her older brother and his friends but they had gone off and left her. They had told her they would come back for her but they had been gone for over two hours. **(H)**

9.2 A Day at the Fair – Possible Courses of Action (1)

(A) Offered a lift by a boy thought to use drink and drugs

Choices:

1. Decide to accept the lift and see what happens.
2. Ignore the boy.
3. Say thanks but refuse the lift.
4. None of the above – your suggestion.

(B) Offered a cigarette by a friend

Choices:

1. Accept the cigarette.
2. Just say 'No thanks'.
3. Tell Kirsty she shouldn't be smoking and to put her cigarette out.
4. None of the above – your suggestion.

(C) Upset by Sam's dangerous driving

Choices:

1. Tell Sam he is an idiot and storm off.
2. Say nothing.
3. Talk to Sam about how upset you are.
4. None of the above – your suggestion.

(D) Recognizing a bag snatcher

Choices:

1. Do nothing – it's none of your business.
2. Call the police on your mobile phone.
3. Wait until you get home and tell your mum.
4. None of the above – your suggestion.

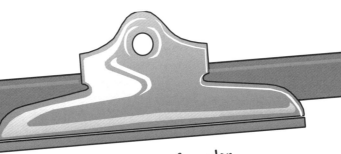

(E) Find some small plastic bags of powder

Choices:

1. Taste the powder to see what it is.
2. Put the plastic bag back in the hole in the tree.
3. Take the bag to the police station.
4. None of the above – your suggestion.

(F) Some boys offer you some alcohol

Choices:

1. Accept just a little of it, just to try.
2. Invite the boys to sit down with you and share their drink.
3. Say 'No thanks'.
4. None of the above – your suggestion.

(G) See some boys assaulting an old man

Choices:

1. Shout to them to leave the man alone.
2. Stand and watch.
3. Call the police on your mobile phone.
4. None of the above – your suggestion.

(H) Find a little girl who has been left by her brother

Choices:

1. Tell the girl to keep waiting.
2. Take the girl over to the nearest adult.
3. Ring home on your mobile phone and ask for advice.
4. None of the above – your suggestion.

Exercise 10

Alcohol Pyramid Ten

Suggested age: 9–10 • Suggested time: 30–40 minutes

Outline

An exercise to encourage participants to examine pressures, temptations and reasons that lead young people to start or to continue using alcohol. It also looks at the corresponding pressures, temptations and reasons that prevent many young people using alcohol or that encourage current users to stop.

Purpose and expected outcome

- To enable the examination of issues that affect alcohol use decisions.
- To place such issues in order of their importance.
- To encourage participants to consider the alcohol decisions of others.
- To challenge attitudes to alcohol use.
- To reinforce safety and healthy living messages.

Method

The worksheets should be copied and cut up to produce sufficient sets for small group work. If it is intended to use the sets repeatedly they can be laminated. The teacher or group leader should briefly outline the purpose of the exercise, and split the class up into small groups. The cards that deal with reasons to start or continue alcohol use should be distributed, one set to each group. Groups should be asked to consider the reasons printed on each card and to select ten of them that, in their opinion, represent the most powerful pressures, temptations or reasons for a young person to start alcohol use or for an existing user to continue. Each set includes a blank card that can be used by the group to include a reason that they feel has been

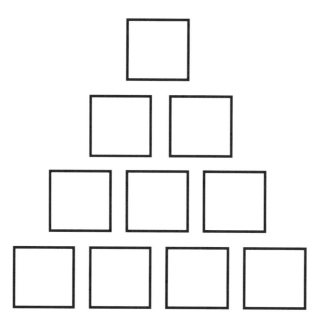

omitted. Having selected ten cards the group should then arrange them in the 'pyramid ten' layout, as shown.

The top position should be occupied by the card that, in the opinion of the group, contains the most important and powerful reason to start or continue alcohol use. The two positions in the second row should be occupied by the cards that contain the next most important or powerful reasons, the third row the three next most important and the bottom row the four cards judged to contain the least important reasons.

When sufficient time has elapsed for each group to arrange its cards in a 'pyramid ten', they should report their choices and placings back to the rest of the class. A simple scoring system can be used to arrive at a common 'pyramid ten'. The card placed at the top by any group should be awarded one point, cards placed in the second row two points, the third row three points and those placed in the bottom row should be awarded four points. Cards not selected for inclusion in any group's 'pyramid ten' should be awarded five points. When all of the groups have reported back, the points can be added up to produce a class 'pyramid ten' shape. The card that scores the lowest number of points should be placed at the top, the next two in the second row and so on until the shape is complete. The two cards that have the highest scores are left out. The teacher can then ask each group why they chose to place a particular card where they did. Groups can also be asked to justify leaving out certain cards or placing them in a lower position. General discussion can then take place.

The cards detailing pressures, temptations and reasons for young people not to start alcohol use, or for existing users to stop their alcohol use, can be used in exactly the same way.

This can be used immediately following the previous 'pyramid ten' exercise or on a separate occasion.

Notes for teacher or group leader

Teachers and group leaders should be sensitive to the possibility that some participants may be adversely affected by some statements within this exercise, due to personal experience.

There are no totally right or wrong answers in this exercise. It is an opportunity for participants to discuss their views and, having come to an agreement, indicate their reasoning. Providing the group has given sufficient thought to the placings and are prepared to explain their reasoning, then any placing order is valid. When a group is unable to agree a particular placing, then a simple vote may resolve the dispute. When a dispute is not resolved by voting, then a separate minority placing order may be accepted. Every effort, however, should be made to achieve agreement.

Follow-up exercises

- Creating a set of reasons for becoming involved in other forms of risk taking and anti-social behaviour, e.g. climbing, canoeing, surfing, theft, vandalism and so on.

- Looking at how such pressures, temptations and reasons exert their influence over young people.

10.1 Reasons to Start or Continue Alcohol Use (1)

To show off to your friends	To get drunk
Everyone is doing it	Pressure from friends
Out of curiosity	The thrill of doing something daring

10.1 Reasons to Start or Continue Alcohol Use (2)

To join in with a group	To give you confidence
To help forget problems	To have a good time
Because just trying it never hurt anyone	

10.2 Reasons to Stop or Not To Start Alcohol Use (1)

Being sick	Friends who don't like it
Parents finding out	Knowing that alcohol can make you ill
A bad hangover	Financial cost

Knowing about alcoholism	Seeing other people's drunken behaviour
Fear of having an accident	Television reports about alcohol problems
Bad effects on your behaviour	

Exercise 11

What's That Rule For?

Suggested age: 10–11 • Suggested time: 45 minutes

Outline

An exercise where small groups of participants discuss the purpose of specific rules that exist in schools. This exercise can also be used in situations other than a school where rules of behaviour apply.

Purpose and expected outcome

- To increase awareness of the reasons that lie behind the rules that are necessary for the good conduct of any society.

- To increase understanding of why society needs rules at all.

- To increase understanding of the importance of complying with such rules.

- To allow participants to listen to the views of their peers, and to formulate and clarify their own views.

- To reinforce safety and healthy living messages.

Method

Dependent on the number and nature of the people in the group, the teacher or group leader will divide the participants into small groups and either ask each to appoint a spokesperson or appoint that person themselves to save time or if felt appropriate. A list of rules that apply within the school are drawn up and a number chosen for further discussion. These can either be divided up between the groups or all groups can discuss all of the rules. The groups should be asked to discuss their understanding of the reasons for the rules and to fit them under one or more of the following headings:

1. To maintain a healthy and safe environment for all school members.
2. To create an environment within which good teaching and learning can be facilitated.
3. To allow everyone to make the most of their time at school.
4. To protect the reputation of the school and its members.
5. To provide finance for certain activities.
6. None of the above.

Following a period of group discussion the spokesperson for each group should report back to the class and a short period of general discussion allowed. Particular discussion should take place of any rules that do not appear to fit under any of the first five of the above headings to attempt to discover the reasons that lie behind these particular rules. Group members should then be asked to suggest laws that exist in society in general that also fit within the above headings, and again to try and think of any laws currently existing that do not fit the first five of the above headings. Any such rules should be particularly discussed to discover the reasons that lie behind them.

Follow-up exercises

Working either singly or in small groups class members should be asked to imagine that they are on the management committee of a youth club that is about to open for young people of their age. They are to create a list of rules for the conduct of the club that fit within one or more of each of the first five headings below. More than one rule for each heading may be created but once the full list has been drawn up they should be placed in order of importance.

- To maintain a healthy and safe environment for all club members.
- To create an environment within which interesting and enjoyable club activities can occur.
- To allow everyone to make the most of their time at the club.
- To protect the reputation of the club and its members.
- To provide finance for certain activities.
- None of the above.

Members should then consider whether any rule needs to be created that does not fit within any of the first five headings.

11.1 School Rules

The following is a list of 12 school rules that have been drawn from a number of different schools. These can be used to prompt discussion amongst the groups as to the validity of each of the rules. The following points could be considered:

- How do they match the rules at your school?

- How do they match up with the list of reasons given above?

- Are they good rules?

- Would you conform to them?

- Could they be improved?

    1. No ball games in the playground before school begins.

    2. Children must line up at the end of playtime.

    3. Children must ask permission to go to the toilet.

    4. Children are not allowed in the stockroom.

    5.   In class we keep our hands and feet to ourselves.

    6. We walk calmly and quietly around the school.

    7. We listen quietly when spoken to by the teacher.

    8. We make sure that no one is ever lonely in the playground.

    9. As soon as the bell is rung all parents should leave the playground.

    10. Children will not wear earrings or studs.

    11. Children must enter the hall in silence.

    12. Children eating packed lunches must take all their litter home with them.

Exercise 12

Get It Straight

Suggested age: 10–11 • Suggested time: 40 minutes

Outline

A quiz in 'true or false' and short answer format, designed to allow participants to check out their knowledge and understanding of substance misuse and other risky behaviours.

This quiz is the third of four such quizzes, one for each age group, contained in this volume. A number of similar questions are to be found in some of the quizzes. This is deliberate and allows for the answers given by participants to become more comprehensive as their maturity and understanding develops.

Purpose and expected outcome

- To provide accurate information about drugs and drug use, alcohol use, smoking and other risky behaviour.

- To encourage thoughtful debate about such issues.

- To encourage good decision making.

- To reinforce safety and healthy living messages.

Method

The quiz consists of 40 questions designed to be suitable for young people aged 10 to 11 years. The first two sheets contain 15 questions each, which all require answers of either 'true' or 'false'. The third sheet has 10 questions which require a mixture of 'true/false' and short paragraph-length answers. The teacher or group leader can decide on the length of the quiz to suit the participants and the time available.

It should be explained to the participants that the purpose of the quiz is not to examine their level of knowledge about such topics as drugs, alcohol, smoking and other forms of risky behaviour but rather to encourage them to consider such issues and check out the

accuracy or otherwise of any knowledge they may already have, and to add useful, accurate and balanced information.

The quiz sheets should be copied and handed out to the participants, and time allowed for them to answer the questions. The teacher or group leader should then go through the answers with the participants using the guidance notes below. Many of the questions will prompt discussion of the question itself and a number of associated issues. This is intended, and should be encouraged.

Participants should be asked to correct their sheets in line with the given answers and keep them for future reference.

Notes for teacher or group leader

Teachers and group leaders should be sensitive to the possibility that some participants may be adversely affected by some statements within this exercise, due to personal experience.

This exercise contains some words and expressions that may be unfamiliar to participants and require further explanation. These include the following:

- prescribed
- mental health
- solvent sniffing
- illegal drug
- aggression
- mountaineering
- potential
- irresponsible
- justified.

Suggested answers

1. **True**. Many prescribed drugs, when misused, can produce non-therapeutic recreational effects such as stimulation, intoxication or sedation. If used for excessive periods of time or in excess dosage, addiction can also result.

2. **True**. Excessive alcohol use can lead to serious damage to mental health. Depression, anxiety, delusions and negative changes in personality can occur. Korsakoff's psychosis occurs in some excessive users of alcohol. This form of dementia results in disorientation, loss of memory and lowered intellectual abilities. It is reversible in some sufferers through the administration of thiamine (vitamin B_1).

3. **False**. In the UK it is illegal to give alcohol to those under five years of age except for medical reasons. It is therefore legal for those over five to drink alcohol at home. However, if parents allowed excessive use, it could be considered a form of neglect or abuse in the eyes of the law.

4. **False**. When someone smokes tobacco, the air becomes contaminated with tobacco smoke over a wide area. This can be particularly dense when several people smoke in the same room. This smoke contains high levels of toxic chemicals and can eventually lead to all of the diseases associated with smoking, even in non-smokers who inhale it.

5. **True**. Smoking is seen by many young people as being a 'grown up' activity.

6. **True**. Sniffing solvents is *highly dangerous*. There is a danger of sudden death caused by overstimulation of the heart or asphyxiation caused by swelling of the throat tissues or inhalation of vomit. Users also expose themselves to a high level of risk of accidents whilst intoxicated.

7. **True**. Cannabis is a depressant drug. One of its effects is to slow you down psychologically (slows brain activity) and, as a result, physically.

8. **False**. In the UK, government statistics for 2004 indicated that 18 per cent of boys between 11 and 15 years of age used illegal drugs in the past year, compared with 17 per cent of girls of the same age. However, in the USA, government statistics issued in February 2006 reported a higher number of teenage girls using cannabis and prescription drugs than teenage boys.

9. **True**. A user of illegal drugs is breaking the law and therefore is a criminal. Many addicted drug users spend large sums of money on their drugs of choice. For many such users this money is raised by theft, drug dealing or prostitution.

10. **False**. Getting drunk on alcohol carries with it a high risk of serious accidents, especially when driving or performing any activity that calls for careful judgement. It can be especially dangerous to young people who may become insensible very quickly and collapse with a high risk of asphyxiation due to inhalation of vomit.

11. **False**. In most cases people will think you are foolish rather than cool.

12. **True**. See answer 4 above.

13. **True**. Many illegal drugs are very impure, containing many contaminating substances. These substances may not dissolve completely and lead to blockages of small blood vessels. Injecting any drug carries the risk of vein collapse and of infections such as HIV/AIDS and hepatitis, if needles and syringes are shared. Once a drug is injected it can not easily be removed from the body, thus any adverse reactions are potentially more dangerous.

14. **True**. Tea, coffee and cola all contain caffeine, a mild stimulant drug. In small quantities it provides a refreshing increase in energy levels and wakefulness; in

larger quantities it can lead to headaches, anxiety, agitation, tremors and insomnia. In extreme cases fatal overdoses have occurred.

15. **False**. Modern trains travel at very high speeds (100 mph = 44.5 m per second) so they can literally be on top of you before you can get clear. Also many train tracks have an electrified third rail which can kill instantly on contact.

16. **False**. Drinking alcohol in sensible moderate quantities may make some people more relaxed. However, excessive consumption of alcohol does lead some people to behave in an unthinking, careless, noisy or aggressive way.

17. **True**. See answer 16 above.

18. **False**. See answer 1 above. Also, some medicinal drugs may not suit everybody; indeed some people have very adverse reactions to particular drugs that others use very safely.

19. **True**. Used needles and syringes are likely to be contaminated with traces of the blood of the user. This blood may carry harmful bacteria or viruses.

20. **True**. Dealing in illegal drugs (or prescribed drugs without authority) is an illegal act. In most countries supplying drugs carries very heavy legal penalties, e.g. in the UK dealing in heroin carries a maximum sentence of life imprisonment.

21. **False**. Nicotine is a highly addictive drug and the 'smoking habit' can be very difficult to stop. Many people have to resort to medication, such as nicotine patches or gum, to help them stop. The best plan is never to start.

22. **False**. Young lungs and other organs are particularly vulnerable to damage by smoking tobacco. Many young people who take up smoking become addicted and continue well into adult life. Smoking decreases oxygen intake which can harm physical and mental development.

23. **False**. These dates have been carefully calculated by the manufacturers and give a good indication of when a medicine is beginning to lose its effectiveness.

24. **True**. Many drugs directly affect the brain and produce changes in mood, sometimes positive, sometimes negative.

25. **False**. There is little evidence to suggest that one form of smoking tobacco is really any 'safer' than any other.

26. **True**. The use of alcohol and many street drugs can lead to a slowing of brain activity and a lowering of the ability to concentrate. It can also affect memory.

27. **True**. Risk taking is a natural part of most young people's personality. Taking risks can be exciting and enjoyable and can enhance personal development. The important thing is to know the exact nature of the risk you are taking and what the possible drawbacks and benefits of taking it are. Also, circumstances may arise when it is necessary to take a risk to achieve something important such as saving someone's life.

28. **True**. A correctly worn seat belt will, in the event of an accident, prevent you being thrown violently forward or to the side resulting in a potentially life-threatening impact with the interior of the car.

29. **True**. See answer 28 above.

30. **False**. This could lead to an explosion and cause serious injury.

31. **False**. An element of risk can make a sport very exciting. However, it is necessary to understand the nature of that risk and take action to control it, such as using appropriate safety equipment.

32. **True**. Most aerosols contain flammable gas under high pressure. They can also explode if burnt, even when apparently empty.

33. **False**. Many wild mushrooms are both safe and delicious to eat; however, there are many highly poisonous varieties. Some of these poisonous varieties look very similar to edible ones. You need expert knowledge to tell the difference.

34. **False**. Why should they? They want you to buy the drug. They will only tell you the good things that you want to hear.

35. **False**. Smoke from a fire can build up very rapidly. Such smoke can be very thick and, in some cases, highly poisonous. You should always evacuate a building in the correct manner on hearing a fire alarm unless told otherwise by a responsible person.

Questions to think about

36. In 2004 in the UK 1136 people were injured in firework accidents, with 515 of them needing hospital treatment. More than half of these casualties were young people under the age of 18. In 2004 in the USA 9600 people were treated for firework injuries in hospital emergency rooms. Many of these accidents could be avoided by following the 'Firework Code':

    1. Keep fireworks in a sealed box or tin.
    2. Use them one at a time, replacing the lid immediately.
    3. *Never* put fireworks in your pocket.
    4. Read the instructions carefully, using a torch or flashlight; *never* use a naked flame.
    5. Light fireworks at arm's length, using a taper or a fireworks lighter.
    6. Stand well back and *never* return to a firework after it has been lit; it could explode in your face.
    7. Ensure that all children with fireworks are well supervised.
    8. *Never* throw fireworks.
    9. Keep all pets and animals indoors.
    10. Take care with sparklers: wear gloves to hold them, and dispose of sparklers in a bucket of water as soon as they are finished.

Organized firework celebrations, to which the public are admitted, have to adhere to stringent safety regulations and may be safer to attend than a private celebration.

37. Taking unnecessary risks may place you and other people in danger. However, see answer 27 above.

38. This is not true. Lifts/elevators are powered by electricity which may fail or be cut off during a fire. The lift will then automatically stop and any occupants would find themselves trapped.

39. For instance, heroin, cocaine, crack, amphetamine, crystal meth (methamphetamine), cannabis, PCP, nicotine, alcohol.

40. Smoke alarms will sound long before the levels of smoke become dangerously high. This provides people with valuable time to evacuate a burning building. Many fires start at night when the occupants of a building are asleep. Smoke alarms will wake such occupants and allow them time to escape.

Follow-up exercises

- The quiz will have raised many issues connected with risky behaviour. Any of these can be followed up with discussions, role-play exercises, story writing, or researching local and national newspapers and magazines.

12.1 Get It Straight (1)

✔

	True	False
1. Some drugs prescribed by your doctor can be misused.	☐	☐
2. Alcohol can affect your mental health.	☐	☐
3. It is illegal to drink alcohol at home if you are under 18.	☐	☐
4. Your health can't be affected by other people smoking.	☐	☐
5. Some young people smoke to look more grown up.	☐	☐
6. Solvent sniffing can kill you.	☐	☐
7. Smoking cannabis can slow you down.	☐	☐
8. More girls use illegal drugs than boys.	☐	☐
9. All illegal drug users are criminals.	☐	☐
10. Getting drunk is fun and harmless.	☐	☐
11. If you tell others that you use drugs people think you're cool.	☐	☐
12. People should not smoke cigarettes in public places.	☐	☐
13. Injecting drugs is the most dangerous way to use them.	☐	☐
14. Tea, coffee and cola can keep you awake.	☐	☐
15. It's safe to cross a railway line as long as you cannot see a train coming.	☐	☐

✔

12.1 Get It Straight (2)

	True	False
16. Drinking alcohol makes some people behave better.	☐	☐
17. Drinking alcohol makes some people behave aggressively.	☐	☐
18. All medicinal drugs are safe to use.	☐	☐
19. Used needles and syringes can spread diseases.	☐	☐
20. Drug dealers are criminals.	☐	☐
21. It's easy to start and to stop smoking.	☐	☐
22. Smoking when you are young is not harmful.	☐	☐
23. Use-by dates on medicines are not really important.	☐	☐
24. People use drugs to change how they feel.	☐	☐
25. Cigars and pipes are safer than cigarettes.	☐	☐
26. Using alcohol or drugs can affect your school work.	☐	☐
27. Taking a risk is sometimes the right thing to do.	☐	☐
28. Seat belts save lives.	☐	☐
29. Trains should have seat belts fitted.	☐	☐
30. It is OK to light a campfire with petrol/gasoline.	☐	☐

12.1 Get It Straight (3)

	True	False
31. Sports such as diving and mountaineering can lead to accidents and therefore should be banned.	☐	☐
32. Aerosol cans are a potential fire hazard.	☐	☐
33. You should never eat wild mushrooms.	☐	☐
34. People who supply illegal drugs will always tell you of any dangers.	☐	☐
35. It is safe to ignore a fire alarm if you do not see a fire or any smoke.	☐	☐

Questions to think about

36. Every year many accidents occur due to the use of fireworks. How might these be avoided?

37. People who take unnecessary risks are irresponsible. When might taking a risk be justified?

38. You should always use the lift/elevator to leave a building quickly where the fire alarm has sounded. Is this true? Give reasons for your answer.

39. Name three addictive drugs.

40. Are smoke alarms in houses really necessary? Give reasons.

Exercise 13

Scenarios 3

Suggested age: 10–11 • Suggested time: 30 minutes

Outline

An exercise to encourage participants to look at the dangers present in a number of different situations and to consider the options available to the people involved.

Purpose and expected outcome

- To enable participants to explore possible ways of avoiding dangerous situations.

- To encourage participants to examine the sources of help that are available to those experiencing difficulties.

- To encourage individual responsibility over decisions involving risk taking.

- To challenge attitudes to anti-social or criminal activities, and drink or drug use.

- To reinforce safety and healthy living messages.

Method

The teacher or group leader should briefly outline the exercise and split the participants into small groups. Each group should be issued with a copy of one of the scenarios. They should then be asked to discuss the scenario and to answer the following questions.

1. How could the person/persons in the scenario have avoided getting into the particular situation?

2. Where could they get help or advice?

3. What are the possible further problems that they might face if the situation does not change?

4. Now they are in the situation, what can they do to change it?

As an alternative the teacher or group leader could read out the scenarios to the participants.

The teacher or group leader should allow sufficient time for the group to consider all of the possibilities in the situation, and then ask them to report back to the rest of the class the various points that they have discussed, and the solutions that they have come up with. The rest of the class can comment upon the points raised and the suggested solutions.

Notes for teacher or group leader

The session leader will need to be aware that some of the participants may be in personal circumstances that are closely similar to those in the scenarios, and will need to be sensitive to this. It may be advisable to remove a particular scenario if this is felt to be too 'close to home' for any member of the group.

This exercise can be used as an individual exercise with pupils being asked to consider and answer one or a number of scenarios, verbally or in writing. As an alternative the teacher can read one of the scenarios to the class and then hold a general discussion on the points that it raises, and take suggested answers from the class to the questions posed earlier.

A list of agencies that might be able to offer help and advice is given in the Useful Organizations and Websites section of this book.

Follow-up exercises

- Pupils can be asked to research and draw up a list of national or local helping agencies that offer advice in these types of situations.

- Pupils can be asked to collect newspaper reports of real-life situations that are similar to those depicted in the scenarios and to discuss them in the same way as they have discussed the scenarios.

13.1 Hannah

Hannah is 11 and thinks she is overweight. Her mother has told her that her weight is normal for a girl of her height and age. Despite this Hannah still thinks she is overweight compared to other girls at her school. She has heard that smoking cigarettes will help her to lose weight and has begun to smoke. She is now smoking four cigarettes every day.

13.2 Jo and Harry

Jo and Harry are both 11. They regularly skip school and spend the day in the local town centre. They hang around the shops and often shoplift food and sweets. They have been chased by security officers on a couple of occasions but have not been caught yet. Jo's older brother has found out about the boys' activities and has threatened Jo that he will tell their parents if they do not steal things for him.

13.3 Gash

Gash is 11 and lives with his parents, one older brother and two younger sisters. Both of his parents use heroin, which they inject, and his father sells cannabis to young people who call at the house. Neither of his parents has a job and their drug use means that there is often little money for food and heating the house. Gash loves his parents very much and does not want them to get into any trouble. He is also very worried about them and is afraid that their drug use will make them very ill. He is getting desperate and does not know what to do.

13.4 Gavin

Gavin is ten and lives at home with both his parents and a sister aged 12. Because his parents both work, Gavin and his sister are alone in the house after school until his mother gets home from work at 5.15pm. One day Gavin has a bad headache at school. He goes to see the school nurse during the afternoon break and she advises him to go home and tell his mother who may give him something for it. Gavin does not tell the nurse that his mother will not be at home when he gets there. When Gavin gets home his headache is still bad and he decides to help himself to headache tablets from where they are kept in the kitchen cupboard. By mistake he takes some of his mother's other medication.

13.5 Megan

Megan is 11 and lives at home with her mother and her brother who is six. Her father is in the navy and is away at sea for long periods. Megan's mother has a busy job and works very hard keeping the house clean and making good meals for her children. Megan loves her mother very much. She has always known that her mother likes to have a few glasses of wine most evenings but has never seen her drunk. Megan now knows her mother is four months pregnant and is worried about what effect her mother's drinking may have on the unborn baby.

13.6 Julio

Over one weekend, Julio's school is badly flooded. Someone broke in and, after putting the plugs in all the washbasins in the upstairs toilets, they turned all the taps on. The overflowing water ruined carpets on both floors and caused large parts of the ground floor ceiling to collapse. Several televisions, some musical instruments and a lot of computer equipment were ruined. The repairs to the school are very expensive. A week later Julio discovers who caused all the damage and the vandals find out that he knows about them.

Exercise 14

Do the Right Thing 3

Suggested age: 10–11 • Suggested time: 40 minutes

Outline

An exercise consisting of a storyline within which are embedded eight different incidents, which require the reader or readers to consider a number of courses of action that could be taken by the characters in the story.

Purpose and expected outcome

- To demonstrate that personal experiences of health and safety situations are commonplace in everyday life.

- To enable participants to consider and explore the implications of a range of varying actions in situations where the health and safety of the individual and others is potentially at risk.

- To reinforce safety and healthy living messages.

Method

The exercise worksheet outlines a story of 'everyday life' in which the characters come across eight separate incidents together with a number of suggested courses of action for each. Participants, whether working singly, in pairs or in small groups, should read through the story, and as they encounter each incident then pause to consider the alternative courses of action provided, or suggest a course of action of their own. As another option, the teacher or group leader could read out the story to the participants, pausing at the relevant points.

The teacher or group leader should decide whether participants are asked to report their chosen action on each individual incident as they are encountered, or report back on all eight incidents after completion of the worksheet. Where participants are working in groups, consideration can be given to appointing a suitable spokesperson for each group.

All participants in this exercise should be given the necessary time and resources to consider their chosen actions and if necessary write them down.

Teachers or group leaders should ask participants to give reasons why they have chosen or rejected different courses of action. Other participants should be encouraged to comment on the chosen courses of action and suggest alternatives if time allows.

Notes for teacher or group leader

Teachers and group leaders should be sensitive to the possibility that some participants may be adversely affected by some incidents within the story due to personal experience.

The following guidance notes pertaining to each situation and the alternative courses of action provided are not intended to be comprehensive and exhaustive. Many of the positive and negative aspects of any of the courses of action will be self-evident, and may arise out of group discussions. The notes are intended as guidance only.

It is worth noting that in many instances a suggested course of action will involve passing information about the actions of others to a responsible adult. This is likely to raise the difficult issue of informing or 'grassing'. Participants may object that they do not want to get their friends 'in trouble' but need to consider that a lack of such action may lead to greater risk and harm to their friends, and others.

Suggested answers

(A) Knowing a friend is sniffing solvents
Choices:

1. Ask them to tell you what it is like.
   May give the questioner some insight into why solvents are being used. This alone, however, is not likely to lead to a cessation of unsafe behaviour.

2. Tell them that they are stupid, as it could be dangerous.
   This course of action is a possibility but will depend on how the message is delivered. Can be a way of showing you disapprove but care for the person's welfare. Remember that peer disapproval can be a very powerful force for change.

3. Ask them if they will let you try it.
   This comment can be seen to condone, even encourage, usage. Solvent abuse is *highly dangerous*. UK government statistics report that more than 1700 people under the age of 18 died as a result of solvent abuse between 1983 and 2000. In 2003 this figure was 51. The greatest number of deaths occur in the age group 14 to 18 but deaths have been reported for children under ten years of age.

4. Authors' suggestion.
   Need to consider that the person's actions may be a serious risk to their health and well-being. It is preferable to inform a responsible adult who will take appropriate action, even if it feels as though you are getting your friend 'into trouble'.

(B) Seeing children getting into a building site
Choices:

1. Shout at them not to go in there for their own safety.
    This is a good reaction as it shows you are aware of the risk factors associated with building sites and that you care for the welfare of others. Note the power of peer disapproval.

2. Wait a while, then follow them in to spy on them.
    This course of action also puts you in potential danger, and who will be aware if you or the others have an accident? Also, the persons being followed may react badly.

3. Report what you have seen at school the next day.
    Possible course of action but may be too late if anybody was at risk on the day. Consider letting a responsible person know sooner.

4. Authors' suggestion.
    Best course of action is to give details of the incident to a responsible adult or even inform the police as soon as possible.

(C) Finding a knife
Choices:

1. Pick it up and see how sharp it is.
    Dangerous – could cause possible harm to self.

2. Pick it up and put it in your bag to take home.
    Dangerous – as above – knife must be given to responsible adult at home as soon as possible. May lead to legal problems if found carrying knife.

3. Pick it up and put it in your bag to take to school to show your friends.
    Dangerous – due to taking a blade into school.

4. Authors' suggestion.
    Consider the safety implications of leaving the knife where it is. Pass the relevant details on to a responsible adult as soon as possible so they can act correctly and arrange for its safe removal.

(D) Seeing some young friends in the park with a bottle of vodka
Choices:

1. Go with them so you can share it.
    Dangerous – young people can be at serious risk of alcohol poisoning and accidents whilst under the influence.

2. Say you are going to tell their parents or a teacher.
    May have a deterrent effect but may also anger your friends leading to conflict.

3. Try and take it away from them.
    Dangerous – you are outnumbered and it may develop into a fight or struggle.

4. Authors' suggestion.
   Pass the details of the incident to a responsible adult as soon as possible to allow them to take any necessary action.

(E) Finding some white powder wrapped in paper, possibly a drug
Choices:

1. Smell and taste it to see what it is.
   Very dangerous – may well be an illegal drug, may be toxic and may have adverse effects on your health and well-being. Also, you may well be committing an illegal act.

2. Keep it and offer it for sale to someone you know.
   Very risky – legal risk to self as it may be an illegal drug. Risk to others if they buy and use it.

3. Give it to a younger friend to try.
   As 2.

4. Authors' suggestion.
   Report your find to a responsible adult as soon as possible in order to have the substance safely removed. If no such person available, collect the substance as safely as possible and then hand to a responsible adult at the first opportunity.

(F) Seeing a car on fire
Choices:

1. Stand nearby to see what happens.
   Very risky as car may explode.

2. Try and put the fire out with whatever is at hand.
   Very risky as may be putting self in danger and see 1 above.

3. Call the fire brigade on your mobile.
   Good move! Leave the dangerous task to the trained and equipped professionals. Keep clear of car and warn others to do so until arrival of fire brigade.

4. Authors' suggestion.
   Questionable whether any other action than 3 above should be attempted.

(G) An older boy smells strongly of alcohol and goes to drive his car
Choices:

1. Try and talk him out of driving.
   Possible course of action, but he may take no notice.

2. Go in the car with him to make sure he remains safe.
   Dangerous – putting self at risk as driving will be impaired.

3. Tell him you will call the police if he drives.
   Possible course of action, but this may cause anger and lead to conflict.

4. Authors' suggestion.
    Best course of action is not to get into the car. Explain your concerns for the driver's safety and that of other road users. Consider informing police of situation to ensure safety of driver and others.

(H) You are given information about someone selling drugs to your friends
Choices:

1. Call the police.
    Possible course of action, but also consider informing any other responsible adult, for example a teacher.

2. Tell the person to stop selling drugs.
    May be effective in some limited cases, depending on your relationship. Also possibly putting yourself at risk of conflict.

3. Tell your friends to stop buying drugs and threaten to report them.
    Possible course of action; makes others aware of your knowledge and shows concern for their well-being and safety. Also demonstrates that you will act firmly to try and prevent drug related harm. Need to consider possible adverse reactions from friends.

4. Authors' suggestion.
    Best course of action is to pass relevant information to a responsible adult as soon as possible, in order for them to take appropriate action to prevent or minimize harm.

Follow-up exercises

- The situations below could be acted out in role play in group work or presented as the subject of assemblies.

- Participants could be asked to create further realistic scenarios and suggest correct courses of action.

- Participants could be asked to research similar incidents reported in the media and discuss the actions taken by those involved and the outcomes.

- Contact could be made with the various emergency services to provide up-to-date information and advice.

14.1 Not Just Another Day!

Aminah had the whole day to herself. She had decided that after breakfast she would call her best friend Katie so that they could meet up for the day.

When Katie answered her phone she seemed a little upset, and told Aminah that another friend of theirs, Rachel, had started to sniff solvents from aerosol cans, and that yesterday she had seemed 'drunk'. Katie said she didn't know what to do, and asked Aminah what she thought, as she didn't want Rachel to get into trouble. **(A)**

After this, the girls agreed to meet outside the local shops. On their way there, Aminah saw some younger children from her school playing outside a building site, where a small factory was being knocked down. As she passed she noticed that the children had managed to prise apart some metal panels that were put up to keep people out of the site and were squeezing themselves through the gap into the site. **(B)**

When she eventually reached the shops, Katie was already waiting outside. They smiled and greeted each other and decided to walk to the park, where they would feed ducks on the pond, and watch squirrels and birds in the trees. They hadn't gone very far, when Katie spotted something shiny by the roadside. It was a knife with a long blade and a black handle. It looked a bit dirty, but she still decided to investigate. **(C)**

As they walked along the path towards the pond, some boys that they knew ran noisily past, laughing and obviously up to no good, they thought. One of them was holding a bottle, containing what looked like water. 'What's that?' asked Aminah. 'Vodka,' replied one of the boys and they ran off towards the trees. Aminah was unhappy about the situation for she knew that alcohol could be dangerous. She couldn't decide what she should do. **(D)**

After this, Katie suggested that they go and buy ice creams, which they both liked. As they passed a wooden bench, they both noticed a small blue bag lying underneath it, and saw that the contents had spilled out. Aminah went over to see if there was any clue as to who had lost it. Amongst the tissues, nailfile, train tickets and make-up, she found a small folded piece of paper which appeared to contain something. She opened up the paper and saw a small amount of white powder. What was it? she wondered and what should she do with it? **(E)**

After finishing their ice creams, the girls decided to make their way along the path through the car park. As they did so, they could smell something burning, and saw a lot of smoke rising in the air. As they got nearer to the smoke, they could see that an old car was on fire, and they noticed the same boys who they had seen earlier, running away. Katie started to run towards the burning car. Aminah held back. **(F)**

'What a day,' thought the girls and carried on into the town where they bought a few items from a shop, magazines, sweets and bottled drinks. Further on down the street, they were passing a bar, when Neil, an older boy who they knew, walked out. Neil was now in sixth form college, and they had heard that he had just broken up with his girlfriend and was very unhappy. They said hello to him. He seemed unsteady on his feet and looked at them strangely. After a moment he said 'Hi', before staggering a few steps towards a nearby car. He smelled strongly of alcohol and fumbled with keys to open the driver's door. Aminah could tell he wasn't fit to drive and wondered what to do. **(G)**

On their way home past the shops, the girls bumped into Trish and Kaisu, who were laughing and looking pleased with themselves. 'We know something about your brother,' said Kaisu to Katie, and she told a story about her older cousin who was out of work, and selling drugs to younger children to make some money. 'He's selling them to lots of kids around here,' said Kaisu. 'What! to my brother?' asked Katie. 'Yes, he is,' said Kaisu. Katie felt frightened and started to cry. She begged Aminah to help her to do something about it. Aminah wasn't sure what to do. **(H)**

Eventually their day out came to an end and each girl went home. Aminah said hello to her mother, stroked her cat, then sat in the armchair to think about all that had happened that day. 'I hope tomorrow is less hectic,' she thought to herself.

14.2 Not Just Another Day – Possible Courses of Action (1)

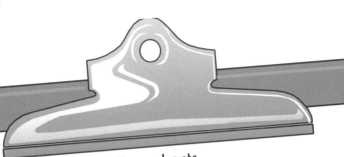

(A) Knowing a friend is sniffing solvents

Choices:

1. Ask them to tell you what it is like.
2. Tell them that they are stupid, as it could be dangerous.
3. Ask them if they will let you try it.
4. None of the above – your suggestion.

(B) Seeing children getting into a building site

Choices:

1. Shout at them not to go in there for their own safety.
2. Wait a while, then follow them in to spy on them.
3. Report what you have seen at school the next day.
4. None of the above – your suggestion.

(C) Finding a knife

Choices:

1. Pick it up and see how sharp it is.
2. Pick it up and put it in your bag to take home.
3. Pick it up and put it in your bag to take to school to show your friends.
4. None of the above – your suggestion.

(D) Seeing some young friends in the park with a bottle of vodka

Choices:

1. Go with them so you can share it.
2. Say that you are going to tell their parents or a teacher.
3. Try and take it away from them.
4. None of the above – your suggestion.

14.2 Not Just Another Day – Possible Courses of Action (2)

(E) Finding some white powder wrapped in paper, possibly a drug

Choices:
1. Smell or taste it to see what it is.
2. Keep it and offer it for sale to someone you know.
3. Give it to a younger friend to try.
4. None of the above – your suggestion.

(F) Seeing a car on fire

Choices:
1. Stand nearby to see what happens.
2. Try and put the fire out with whatever is at hand.
3. Call the fire brigade on your mobile.
4. None of the above – your suggestion.

(G) An older boy smells strongly of alcohol and goes to drive his car

Choices:
1. Try and talk him out of driving.
2. Go in the car with him to make sure he remains safe.
3. Tell him you will call the police if he drives.
4. None of the above – your suggestion.

(H) You are given information about someone selling drugs to your friends

Choices:
1. Call the police.
2. Tell the person to stop selling drugs.
3. Tell your friends to stop buying drugs and threaten to report them.
4. None of the above – your suggestion.

Exercise 15

Smoking Pyramid Ten

Suggested age: 10–11 • Suggested time: 30–40 minutes

Outline

An exercise to encourage participants to examine pressures, temptations and reasons that lead young people to start smoking cigarettes. It also looks at the corresponding pressures, temptations and reasons that prevent many young people smoking or that encourage current smokers to stop.

Purpose and expected outcome

- To enable the examination of issues that affect smoking decisions.

- To place such issues in order of their importance.

- To encourage participants to consider the smoking decisions of others.

- To challenge attitudes to smoking.

- To reinforce safety and healthy living messages.

Method

The worksheets should be copied and cut up to produce sufficient sets for small group work. If it is intended to use the sets repeatedly they can be laminated. The teacher or group leader should briefly outline the purpose of the exercise, and split the class up into small groups. The cards that deal with reasons to start or continue smoking should be distributed, one set to each group. Groups should be asked to consider the reasons printed on each card and to select ten of them that, in their opinion, represent the most powerful pressures, temptations or reasons for a young person to start smoking or for an existing smoker to continue. Each set includes a blank card that can be used by the group to include a reason that they feel has been

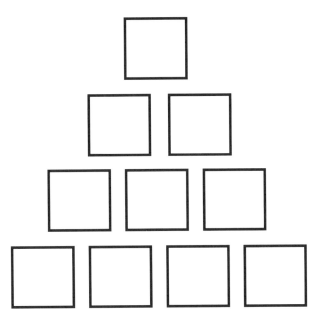

omitted. Having selected ten cards the group should then arrange them in the 'pyramid ten' layout, as shown.

The top position should be occupied by the card that, in the opinion of the group, contains the most important and powerful reason to start or continue smoking. The two positions in the second row should be occupied by the cards that contain the next most important or powerful reasons, the third row the three next most important and the bottom row the four cards judged to contain the least important reasons.

When sufficient time has elapsed for each group to arrange its cards in a 'pyramid ten', they should report their choices and placings back to the rest of the class. A simple scoring system can be used to arrive at a common 'pyramid ten'. The card placed at the top by any group should be awarded one point, cards placed in the second row two points, the third row three points and those placed in the bottom row should be awarded four points. Cards not selected for inclusion in any group's 'pyramid ten' should be awarded five points. When all of the groups have reported back, the points can be added up to produce a class 'pyramid ten' shape. The card that scores the lowest number of points should be placed at the top, the next two in the second row and so on until the shape is complete. The two cards that have the highest scores are left out. The teacher can then ask each group why they chose to place a particular card where they did. Groups can also be asked to justify leaving out certain cards or placing them in a lower position. General discussion can then take place.

The cards detailing pressures, temptations and reasons for young people not to start smoking, or for existing smokers to stop, can be used in exactly the same way.

This can be used immediately following the previous 'pyramid ten' exercise or on a separate occasion.

Notes for teacher or group leader

Teachers and group leaders should be sensitive to the possibility that some participants may be adversely affected by some statement within this exercise, due to personal experience.

There are no totally right or wrong answers in this exercise. It is an opportunity for participants to discuss their views and, having come to an agreement, indicate their reasoning. Providing the group has given sufficient thought to the placings and are prepared to explain their reasoning, then any placing order is valid. When a group is unable to agree a particular placing, then a simple vote may resolve the dispute. When a dispute is not resolved by voting, then a separate minority placing order may be accepted. Every effort, however, should be made to achieve agreement.

This exercise contains some words and expressions that may be unfamiliar to participants and require further explanation. These include the following:

- curiosity
- disapprove
- impress
- financial cost
- hooked.

Follow-up exercises

- Creating a set of reasons for becoming involved in other forms of risk taking or anti-social behaviour, e.g. vandalism, theft, drug use, skateboarding, BMX trick riding, and so on.

- Looking at how such pressures, temptations and reasons exert their influence over young people.

15.1 Reasons to Start or Continue Smoking (1)

For pleasure	To be like your parents
Because everyone is doing it	Pressure from friends
Out of curiosity	The thrill of doing something daring

15.1 Reasons to Start or Continue Smoking (2)

To join in
with a group

To give you
confidence

To help forget
problems

To have a
good time

Because just
trying it never
hurt anyone

15.2 Reasons to Stop or Not to Start Smoking (1)

The risks to health	A friend who disapproves of smoking
Parents finding out	Getting caught by a teacher
A relative who died from a smoking disease	Financial cost

Smelly breath and clothing	Need to be fit for sport or other interest
A school health education class about smoking	Fear of becoming hooked on cigarettes
Friends at school say you look stupid	

Exercise 16

Life – A Risky Business

Suggested age: 11–12 • Suggested time: 40 minutes

Outline

An exercise comprising individual statements, some describing everyday events and others more unusual, designed to increase participants' awareness and understanding of the risk assessment procedure, both for themselves and others.

Purpose and expected outcome

- To introduce the concept of risk assessment.

- To enable participants to consider risk to self and the wider risk to others.

- To encourage forward thinking and the consideration of possible outcomes.

- To reinforce safety and healthy living messages.

Method

This exercise comprises 30 statements, some depicting normal everyday scenarios, whilst others are less usual. Depending on the time available, the number of participants and their considered ability, the exercise statements can be given out individually, to small groups, pairs, or considered by the entire group. The group leader should explain that participants are to decide whether there is any potential risk in the action described, first to the individual, and second to any other person or persons. They are then to try and agree on the degree of risk as being:

1. no risk

2. some risk to self or others

3. moderate risk to self or others

4. high risk to self or others.

The teacher or group leader should encourage discussion and once agreement has been made or a democratic vote taken the statements can be placed into ballot type boxes labelled with the four different risk levels. As a further enhancement the boxes can be coloured as follows: Risk Level One – Green; Level Two – Yellow; Level Three – Orange; Level Four – Red.

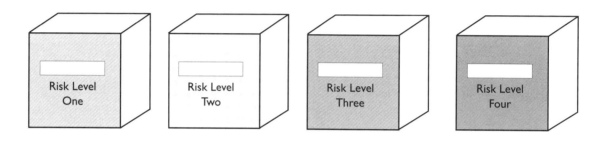

Statements should be given out randomly, or selected by participants, and time allowed for consideration and debate before the participants are asked in turn to read out their statement to the rest of the group, reflect on their discussion or consideration and then categorize the statement as Risk Level 1, 2, 3 or 4, based on their deliberations. If unsure about the level of risk, the teacher or group leader could assist or ask for help from other participants in the group. If the degree of risk has not been fully considered or there is disagreement, the group leader may wish to intervene to resolve the situation or the statement could be held over for consideration at another time.

Notes for teacher or group leader

Almost any action that we take in life can have its consequences and risks, even if they are hidden from us at the time.

Many of the statements in this exercise contain obvious and immediate risks and consequences to the person carrying out the action, or to others, whilst for some statements the risks and consequences are less obvious, especially for young people. Some actions may even seem exciting and attractive due to the risk content, or because of the challenge of a dare, or just to impress others.

Teachers and group leaders should be sensitive to the possibility that some participants may have experienced the risks and consequences of similar actions by themselves or others, and withdraw certain statements before the exercise begins.

Follow-up exercises

- Collecting media articles on similar incidents to those outlined in the exercise.

- Writing a story involving one or more of the situations in this exercise.

- Further group discussion of issues raised during this exercise.

16.1 Statements (1)

✂

1. Run on to busy road without looking to pick up a personal item.

✂

2. Use a mobile phone.

3. Pick up a needle and syringe from the street and put it in your pocket or pencil case.

4. Take more headache tablets at one time than is recommended on the packet.

5. Play with petrol and matches.

6. Smoke an unusual cigarette given to you by a friend's older sister.

7. Take someone else's medicine without anyone knowing.

8. Eat a banana and throw away the skin.

9. Eat food containing peanuts when you think you may be allergic to them.

10. Swallow tablets that a friend tells you will make you feel happy.

11. Steal a bottle of vodka and drink it with your friends.

12. Sniff solvents alone in a shed.

13. Steal and hide a friend's asthma inhaler as a joke.

14. Steal money from a parent's bag, purse or wallet.

15. Run away from a friend who collapsed after using drugs, because you are scared.

16.1 Statements (2)

16. Go with a stranger who says he wants you to help him.

17. Pick up a live wasp.

18. Get into a car with a driver you believe to be drunk.

19. Eat 27 chocolate bars in one go.

20. Take a drink of yellow liquid you found in a discarded lemonade bottle.

21. Dare a friend to walk on a frozen pond.

22. Ride a bike at night on the road without lights.

23. Eat a yoghurt that is three weeks out of date.

24. Taste some white powder that you found hidden in your brother's bedroom.

25. Drink three litres of cola.

26. Stroke a snarling dog that is eating a bone.

27. Eat a cake that you are told contains cannabis.

28. Walk through a dark cemetery alone at night.

29. Swallow a live worm.

30. Never clean your teeth.

Exercise 17

The Truth Is Out There!

Suggested age: 11–12 • Suggested time: 40 minutes

Outline

A quiz in 'true or false' and short answer format, designed to allow participants to check out their knowledge and understanding of substance misuse and other risky behaviours.

This quiz is the last of four such quizzes, one for each age group, contained in this volume. A number of similar questions are to be found in some of the quizzes. This is deliberate and allows for the answers given by participants to become more comprehensive as their maturity and understanding develops.

Purpose and expected outcome

- To provide accurate information about drugs and drug use, alcohol use, smoking and other risky behaviour.

- To encourage thoughtful debate about such issues.

- To encourage good decision making.

- To reinforce safety and healthy living messages.

Method

The quiz consists of 60 questions designed to be suitable for young people aged 11 to 12 years. The first three sheets contain 15 questions each, which all require answers of either 'true' or 'false'. The fourth sheet has 15 questions which require a mixture of 'true/false' and short paragraph-length answers. The teacher or group leader can decide on the length of the quiz to suit the participants and the time available.

It should be explained to the participants that the purpose of the quiz is not to examine their level of knowledge about such topics as drugs, alcohol, smoking and other forms of risky behaviour but rather to encourage them to consider such issues and check out the

accuracy or otherwise of any knowledge they may already have, and to add useful, accurate and balanced information.

The quiz sheets should be copied and handed out to the participants, and time allowed for them to answer the questions. The teacher or group leader should then go through the answers with the participants, using the guidance notes below. Many of the questions will prompt discussion of the question itself and a number of associated issues. This is intended, and should be encouraged.

Participants should be asked to correct their sheets in line with the given answers and keep them for future reference.

Notes for teacher or group leader

Teachers and group leaders should be sensitive to the possibility that some participants may be adversely affected by some statements within this exercise, due to personal experience.

Suggested answers

1. **False.** Drugs prescribed by a doctor can be very good for your health; however, it should be remembered that even drugs prescribed by the doctor can be harmful if misused. Also it is sometimes possible for a patient to have an adverse reaction to a prescribed drug that they used in accordance with the doctor's instructions.

2. **False.** Alcohol can be safely used by adults in sensible moderate amounts. However, when used in excess it can lead to a wide range of physical and mental problems, e.g. heart and liver disease, cancers, increased risk of stroke, mood and personality changes and dementia (Korsakoff's psychosis).

3. **True.** Alcohol impairs the skilful judgements needed to drive safely. It is illegal in most countries to drive on the road with more than a set amount of alcohol in your bloodstream.

4. **True.** Taking a mix of drugs at the same time can be *very dangerous*. The effects of one drug can be magnified or altered by those of another drug, with very unpredictable results.

5. **True.** See answer 2 above. However, it is sometimes recommended that elderly people use one or two units of alcohol a day to aid circulation and therefore improve general health.

6. **True.** A large number of chemical compounds are released by the burning of tobacco. Amongst them are the following toxic substances: carbon monoxide, hydrogen cyanide, nitrogen oxide, ammonia, sulphur dioxide, hydrogen sulphide and toluene.

7. **True**. When someone smokes tobacco, the air becomes contaminated with tobacco smoke over a wide area. This can be particularly dense when several people smoke in the same room. This smoke contains high levels of toxic chemicals and can eventually lead to all the diseases associated with smoking in non-smokers who breathe this toxic smoke.

8. **True**. Smoking tobacco can decrease one's appetite. However, the dangerous risk to health brought about by smoking far outweighs any health benefits of losing excess weight.

9. **False**. Whilst it is true that the teacher or group leader is responsible for your safety, you are still fully responsible for the safety of yourself and those around you.

10. **True**. Sniffing solvents is *highly dangerous*. There is a danger of sudden death caused by overstimulation of the heart or asphyxiation caused by swelling of the throat tissues or inhalation of vomit. Users also expose themselves to a high level of risk of accidents whilst intoxicated.

11. **False**. Cannabis is a depressant drug which achieves its effects by slowing brain activity. This slows the user down both psychologically and physically.

12. **False**. In the UK cannabis is currently a class C controlled drug and illegal to possess.

13. **True**. In low dosages nicotine has the effect of causing relaxation in users. In higher doses agitation and anxiety may result. More usually, people feel they relax by smoking a cigarette as they are topping up nicotine levels and thus stopping withdrawal symptoms from their last use.

14. **True**. In the UK in the early 1980s equal proportions of boys and girls between 11 and 15 years of age smoked regularly. In 2004, 10 per cent of girls were regular smokers compared with 7 per cent of boys. Government statistics released in February 2006 in the USA indicated that the percentage of teenage girls who were regular smokers surpassed that of boys.

15. **True**. Any user of illegal drugs is breaking the law and is therefore a criminal. Many addicted drug users spend large sums of money on their drugs of choice. For many such users this money is raised by theft, drug dealing or prostitution. Dealing in illegal drugs (or prescribed drugs without authority) is an illegal act. In most countries supplying drugs carries very heavy legal penalties, e.g. in the UK dealing in heroin carries a maximum sentence of life imprisonment.

16. **True**. Alcohol impairs judgement and motor co-ordination and leads to many accidents, in the home, on the roads and elsewhere.

17. **True**. See answer 15 above.

18. **False**. UK government statistics for 2004 indicated that 18 per cent of young people between 11 and 15 years of age had used an illegal drug in the previous

12 months. USA government statistics for 2004 indicated that rates of drug use among youths aged 12 to 17 were closely associated with age. The rates of current illicit drug use increased from 3.8 per cent at ages 12 or 13 to 8.9 per cent at ages 14 or 15, and to 17 per cent at ages 16 or 17.

19. **False**. Most street drugs contain contaminating substances. These have either been added deliberately to 'bulk' out the drug or have been left in as a result of inadequate manufacturing processes. Sometimes the contaminants can be extremely harmful to health.

20. **False**. You may just look foolish and sad. However, long-term smoking can prematurely age your skin.

21. **True**. Used needles and syringes are likely to be contaminated with traces of the blood of the user. This blood may carry harmful bacteria or viruses.

22. **True**. Caffeine is a mild stimulant that in moderate dosage does little harm and provides a 'lift'. When taken in excess it can have an adverse effect on heart rate. In very extreme cases fatal overdoses have occurred.

23. **True**. Whilst few people would become addicted to a drug from one use of it, it is worth remembering that every addict started with just trying it the once.

24. **False**. Whilst it is true that smokers and drinkers seem to socialize frequently together and often welcome new 'users' into their company, it is still possible to make as many friends amongst non-'users'. It does not seem worth while making friends at the expense of your health.

25. **False**. Whilst it is true that drug users often make most of their friends amongst other drug users (see answer 24 above), many also have friends who are not users.

26. **True**. Tobacco smoke is considered in most countries to be the most common cause of lung diseases such as cancer and emphysema.

27. **True**. Excessive consumption of alcohol does lead some people to behave in an unthinking, careless, noisy or aggressive way that can, and does, often result in fights.

28. **True**. Headache tablets are safe for most people when used in the correct dosage. There are some people who experience adverse reactions to certain headache tablets. Overuse, however, can lead to serious health problems and even be fatal in extreme cases.

29. **False**. All medicines have to be used according to the manufacturer's instructions. Excessive dosage of many shop-bought medicines can lead to severe overdose problems.

30. **True**. See answer 21 above.

31. **False**. In January 2007 the UK government announced its intention to raise the minimum age at which a person may legally purchase tobacco or tobacco related

products from 16 to 18 years. This change is scheduled to take effect in October 2007. In the USA the minimum age at which cigarettes may be purchased is 18 years.

32. **True**. Using illegal drugs can seriously affect your health, can cost you a lot of money and may lead you to into serious trouble with the law. That doesn't seem like a thing that smart people would do.

33. **True**. Illegal drug habits are a major cause of crime (see answer 15 above) which cost UK citizens many millions of pounds annually. The cost to UK health services likewise runs into many millions of pounds, all paid for out of public funds.

34. **False**. Nicotine is a highly addictive drug and the 'smoking habit' can be very difficult to stop. Many people have to resort to medication, such as nicotine patches or gum, to help them stop. The best way to stop is never to start.

35. **False**. Smoking cigarettes causes damage to the lungs that makes them less efficient, and thus less able to pass oxygen into the bloodstream to power the muscles. Carbon monoxide gas in tobacco smoke takes the place of oxygen being carried in a smoker's blood and provides no nourishment to muscles.

36. **False**. Use-by dates have been carefully calculated by manufacturers to indicate how long a product can be stored before it becomes less safe to eat. Poor storage can shorten this 'shelf life'.

37. **False**. A real friend is someone who cares about you. They will certainly do all that they can to keep you from harming yourself.

38. **True**. Performance-enhancing drugs are used in many sports by athletes who wish to beat their opponents unfairly. Many of these drugs carry serious health risks for the user, and can lead to disqualification and loss of reputation.

39. **True**. Many users of drugs become 'tolerant' to them. This means that more and more of the drug needs to be taken to achieve the desired effects. Also, more drugs equals more cost.

40. **True**. Smokers rapidly become addicted to tobacco. They will smoke every day, seven days each week, 52 weeks each year. If a pack of cigarette costs £5 and they smoke one pack every day, that habit will cost them £1825 each year, and they will have nothing but impaired health to show for it.

41. **True**. Dealing in illegal drugs (or prescribed drugs without authority) is an illegal act. See answer 15 above.

42. **True**. See answer 32 above.

43. **True**. See answer 7 above.

44. **True**. Alcohol and many other drugs can affect judgement and motor co-ordination, and may make the user overly confident. These effects can make a user much more likely to have or cause an accident.

45. **False**. Risk taking is a natural part of most young people's personality. Taking risks can be exciting and enjoyable and can enhance personal development. The important thing is to know the exact nature of the risk you are taking and what the possible drawbacks and benefits of it are. Also, circumstances may arise when it is necessary to take a risk to achieve something important such as saving someone's life.

46. **False**. Carbon monoxide alarms are only needed in homes that use gas (either mains or bottled), oil or solid fuel for heating or cooking. The burning of such products produces carbon monoxide which, if an appliance is faulty, can escape into the atmosphere. Carbon monoxide is a colourless, odourless gas that is highly poisonous and can cause death.

47. **False**. It is illegal in most countries to carry a knife for self-protection. In the UK it is only permitted to carry a folding knife with a blade no longer than three inches, for general use. Any person found to be carrying any form of fixed blade knife must be able to demonstrate a suitable reason for doing so. The following are especially forbidden in the UK. *Flick knives* are knives where the blade is hidden inside the handle and shoots out when a button is pressed. These are also called switchblades or automatic knives. *Butterfly knives* are knives where the blade is hidden inside a handle that splits in two around it, like wings. The handles swing around the blade to open or close it. *Disguised knives* are knives where the blade is hidden inside something like a belt buckle or a fake mobile phone. In the USA the laws relating to the carrying of knives vary from state to state.

48. **False**. Petrol is highly flammable. Using it to start a barbecue could lead to an explosion and cause serious injury.

49. **False**. Fireworks do cause a large number of fires and injury accidents every year. However, if the user follows the Firework Code it is possible to enjoy them with an acceptable level of safety. A non-safety argument for banning them could be made on the grounds that their use often frightens animals and annoys nearby residents.

50. **True**. Firedoors are designed to prevent the flow of oxygen containing air to a fire. Restricting that flow will starve the fire of oxygen and prevent it growing. Propping them open allows any fire to spread easily.

51. **False**. Many wild mushrooms are both safe and delicious to eat; however, there are many highly poisonous varieties. Some of these poisonous varieties look very similar to edible ones. You need expert knowledge to tell the difference, and therefore remain safe.

52. **False**. See answer 4 above.

53. **False**. See answer 45 above.

54. **False**. Smoke from a fire can build up very rapidly. Such smoke can be very thick and, in some cases, highly poisonous. You should always evacuate a building in the correct manner on hearing a fire alarm as soon as possible, unless told otherwise by a responsible person.

55. **True**. But only if this can be done in safety. A small fire may be extinguished with little risk to oneself; however, if in doubt it is safer to get out quickly and call the fire brigade.

Questions to think about

56. Legal: nicotine, caffeine, alcohol, a number of sleeping tablets and tranquillizers. Illegal: heroin, cocaine, crack, cannabis, amphetamine, crystal meth (methamphetamine).

57. • road and track cycle racing – head protection

   • BMX trick riding – head, elbow and knee protection

   • skateboarding – as above

   • motor racing – head protection plus fireproof clothing

   • soccer – shin protection

   • cricket – head, face, leg, arm, hand, chest and groin protection

   • ice hockey goal-keeping – full body protection

   With the exception of the fireproof clothing in motor racing, all the protective clothing listed above is to protect the wearer during collisions with the ground, other players or objects used during play.

58. Lighted candles are only dangerous if they can ignite nearby flammable materials. They should never be left unattended or placed on or near anything that could ignite. All naked flames present a possible fire hazard.

59. Smoke alarms will sound long before the levels of smoke become dangerously high. This provides people with valuable time to evacuate a burning building. Many fires start at night when the occupants of a building are asleep. Smoke alarms, if positioned correctly, will wake such occupants and allow them time to escape. It is necessary to check smoke alarm batteries on a regular basis to ensure they are working.

60. People who supply illegal drugs are usually doing it to raise money, often to finance their own drug habit. They have little interest in the well-being of their customers, only in relieving them of their money. They will say anything necessary to entice someone to part with their money.

Follow-up exercises

- The quiz will have raised many issues connected with risky behaviour. Any of these can be followed up with discussions, role-play exercises, story writing, or researching local and national newspapers and magazines.

✔

17.1 The Truth Is Out There (1)

	True	False
1. Prescribed drugs are good for everyone.	☐	☐
2. Alcohol is a safe drug.	☐	☐
3. It is illegal to drink and drive.	☐	☐
4. Using different drugs at the same time can be especially dangerous.	☐	☐
5. Alcohol can be bad for your health.	☐	☐
6. Tobacco smoke contains poisonous gases and chemicals.	☐	☐
7. Your health can be affected by passive smoking.	☐	☐
8. Smoking can help you to control your weight.	☐	☐
9. When on school trips, your teacher is totally responsible for your personal safety.	☐	☐
10. Sniffing solvents can be deadly.	☐	☐
11. Smoking cannabis makes you smarter.	☐	☐
12. It's legal to smoke cannabis.	☐	☐
13. Smoking cigarettes calms you down.	☐	☐
14. More girls than boys smoke.	☐	☐
15. All illegal drug dealers and users are criminals.	☐	☐

17.1 The Truth Is Out There (2)

	True	False
16. Getting drunk can lead to accidents.	☐	☐
17. Some drug addicts steal to pay for their drugs.	☐	☐
18. All young people try illegal drugs at least once.	☐	☐
19. Street drugs are very pure.	☐	☐
20. If you smoke cigarettes you look older.	☐	☐
21. Injecting drugs can spread diseases such as HIV.	☐	☐
22. Too much caffeine can adversely affect your heart.	☐	☐
23. Trying drugs just once can lead to addiction.	☐	☐
24. You can make more friends if you smoke and drink.	☐	☐
25. Drug users only have other drug users as friends.	☐	☐
26. Cigarette smoke can damage lungs.	☐	☐
27. Many fights are caused by people using alcohol.	☐	☐
28. It's safe to use headache tablets.	☐	☐
29. You cannot overdose on shop-bought medicine.	☐	☐
30. You should never pick up discarded needles and syringes.	☐	☐

✓

17.1 The Truth Is Out There (3)

	True	False
31. Fifteen-year-olds are allowed to buy cigarettes in a shop for an adult.	☐	☐
32. Smart people don't use illegal drugs.	☐	☐
33. Drug habits cost the country a lot of money.	☐	☐
34. It's easy to give up smoking.	☐	☐
35. Smoking does not affect your fitness for sport.	☐	☐
36. Use-by dates on food can safely be ignored.	☐	☐
37. A real friend will not try to stop you using illegal drugs.	☐	☐
38. Some people use drugs to improve their sporting performance.	☐	☐
39. Drug habits can become more and more expensive.	☐	☐
40. Cigarettes are a waste of money.	☐	☐
41. Supplying drugs can lead to a prison sentence and a criminal record.	☐	☐
42. Only losers use illegal drugs.	☐	☐
43. Smoking is an anti-social habit.	☐	☐
44. Alcohol or drug use can cause accidents.	☐	☐
45. Risk taking can never be justified.	☐	☐

17.1 The Truth Is Out There (4)

	True	False
46. All homes need carbon monoxide alarms for safety.	☐	☐
47. You are allowed to carry a knife for self-protection.	☐	☐
48. It is perfectly safe to start a barbecue with petrol/gasoline.	☐	☐
49. All fireworks should be banned because they cause accidents.	☐	☐
50. Firedoors should never be propped open.	☐	☐
51. All mushrooms are safe to eat.	☐	☐
52. Using several drugs at once can be more exciting.	☐	☐
53. Sensible people never take risks.	☐	☐
54. If you hear a fire alarm you should not leave a building before being told to do so.	☐	☐
55. If you discover a fire you should try to extinguish it.	☐	☐

Questions to think about

56. Name three legal and three illegal drugs which can be addictive.

57. Name three sports where protective clothing is worn. What parts of the body do they protect? What might happen if such clothing is not used?

58. Lighted candles are dangerous. Is this true; if so, why?

59. What are the benefits of smoke alarms in houses?

60. Why can't people who supply illegal drugs be totally trusted?

Exercise 18

Scenarios 4

Suggested age: 11–12 • Suggested time: 30 minutes

Outline

An exercise to encourage participants to look at the dangers present in a number of different situations and to consider the options available to the people involved.

Purpose and expected outcome

- To enable participants to explore possible ways of avoiding dangerous situations.

- To encourage participants to examine the sources of help that are available to those experiencing difficulties.

- To encourage individual responsibility over decisions involving risk taking.

- To challenge attitudes to anti-social or criminal activities, and drink or drug use.

- To reinforce safety and healthy living messages.

Method

The teacher or group leader should briefly outline the exercise and split the participants into small groups. Each group should be issued with a copy of one of the scenarios. They should then be asked to discuss the scenario and to answer the following questions.

1. How could the person/persons in the scenario have avoided getting into the particular situation?

2. Where could they get help or advice?

3. What are the possible further problems that they might face if the situation does not change?

4. Now they are in the situation, what can they do to change it?

The teacher or group leader should allow sufficient time for the group to consider all of the possibilities in the situation, and then ask them to report back to the rest of the class the various points that they have discussed, and the solutions that they have come up with. The rest of the class can comment upon the points raised and the suggested solutions.

Notes for teacher or group leader

The session leader will need to be aware that some of the participants may be in personal circumstances that are closely similar to those in the scenarios, and will need to be sensitive to this. It may be advisable to remove a particular scenario if this is felt to be too 'close to home' for any member of the group.

This exercise can be used as an individual exercise with pupils being asked to consider and answer one or a number of scenarios, verbally or in writing. As an alternative the teacher can read one of the scenarios to the class and then hold a general discussion on the points that it raises, and take suggested answers from the class to the questions posed earlier.

A list of agencies that might be able to offer help and advice is given in the Useful Organizations and Websites section of this book.

Follow-up exercises

- Pupils can be asked to research and draw up a list of national or local helping agencies that offer advice in these types of situations.

- Pupils can be asked to collect newspaper reports of real-life situations that are similar to those depicted in the scenarios and to discuss them in the same way as they have discussed the scenarios.

18.1 Mitchell

Mitchell is 12 and has been smoking regularly for about a year. One day one of his older brother's friends offers him some cannabis to smoke. Mitchell's brother tells him that it is harmless and that he and his friends all smoke it.

18.2 Crystal and Joni

Crystal is 12 and regularly steals from the shops in the shopping centre. She sometimes sells stolen things at her school. Some of the other pupils ask her to steal them particular things and they pay her for them. Joni is also 12 and tells her mother about Crystal. Joni's mother tells her to ask Crystal to get her some expensive perfume and she will pay her.

18.3 Harry

Harry is 11 and is a bit of a loner at school. He does not find it easy to make friends and often spends a lot of his time on his own. One day he is sitting by himself near the school fence during break time when he sees some of the other boys in his class meeting an older boy close to the other side of the fence. They do not see him and as he watches they appear to give the boy some money in return for a plastic bag that contains what Harry thinks looks like cannabis. The boys then return to school.

18.4 Robain

Robain is 11 and has recently moved to live in this country with his parents and younger brother. His English is steadily improving but he still has a noticeable accent and sometimes has difficulty making himself understood. He had a lot of friends in his former country and wants to make friends here. He tries to join in with a group of other boys but they make fun of the way he speaks. He persists and eventually the leader of this group tells him that he can join them if he pays a forfeit first. He tells Robain that he must steal a big bottle of cider from the local shop for them all to share.

18.5 Kalvin

Kalvin is 11 and recently joined a junior karate club. He soon finds that he does not like the club. The staff often swear at the young members when they don't perform a move correctly, and on several occasions Kalvin has seen one particular member of staff slapping members for making mistakes. Kalvin tries to tell his father about what is happening and that he wants to leave. His father gets cross with him and calls him a sissy. He tells Kalvin that the club will do him good and toughen him up.

18.6 Angel

Angel is 12 and a member of the local swimming club. She is a good swimmer and has won a number of medals for backstroke and butterfly stroke events. The staff at the club tell her and her parents that she could make it to international or even Olympic level if she is prepared to train very hard. One day her personal coach at the club suggests to her that she take some special tablets that will help her build up her muscles. He tells her that they are only 'food supplement' tablets but also tells her that she should not tell anyone else about them, not even her parents.

Exercise 19

Do the Right Thing 4

Suggested age: 11–12 • Suggested time: 40 minutes

Outline

An exercise consisting of a storyline within which are embedded eight different incidents, which require the reader or readers to consider a number of courses of action that could be taken by the characters in the story.

Purpose and expected outcome

- To demonstrate that personal experiences of health and safety situations are commonplace in everyday life.

- To enable participants to consider and explore the implications of a range of varying actions in situations where the health and safety of the individual and others is potentially at risk.

- To reinforce safety and healthy living messages.

Method

The exercise worksheet outlines a story of 'everyday life' in which the characters come across eight separate incidents together with a number of suggested courses of action for each. Participants, whether working singly, in pairs or in small groups, should read through the story, and as they encounter each incident pause to consider the alternative courses of action provided, or suggest a course of action of their own. As another option, the teacher or group leader could read out the story to the participants, pausing at the relevant parts.

   The teacher or group leader should decide whether participants are asked to report their chosen action on each individual incident as they are encountered, or report back on all eight incidents after completion of the worksheet. Where participants are working in groups, consideration can be given to appointing a spokesperson for each group.

All participants in this exercise should be given the necessary time and resources to consider their chosen actions and if necessary write them down.

Teachers or group leaders should ask participants to give reasons why they have chosen or rejected different courses of action. Other participants should be encouraged to comment on the chosen courses of action and suggest alternatives if time allows.

Notes for teacher or group leader

Teachers and group leaders should be sensitive to the possibility that some participants may be adversely affected by some incidents within the story due to personal experience.

The following guidance notes pertaining to each situation, and the alternative courses of action provided, are not intended to be comprehensive and exhaustive. Many of the positive and negative aspects of any of the courses of action will be self-evident, and may arise out of group discussions. The notes are intended as guidance only.

It is worth noting that in many instances a suggested course of action will involve passing information about the actions of others to a responsible adult. This is likely to raise the difficult issue of informing or 'grassing'. Participants may object that they do not want to get their friends 'in trouble' but need to consider that a lack of such action may lead to greater risk and harm to their friends, and others.

Suggested answers

(A) Finding a used and discarded needle and syringe
Choices:

1. Pick it up and put it in the nearest waste bin.
    Dangerous – may be infected and cause accidental harm. Also dangerous to anybody emptying the waste bin.

2. Pick it up and put it in your pocket for later.
    Dangerous – may be infected and cause accidental harm, especially when you try to retrieve it. May pierce clothing and you!

3. Pick it up and chase your friends with it.
    Dangerous – may be infected and cause accidental harm. May harm friends or self if you collide or trip.

4. Authors' suggestion.
    Immediately inform a responsible adult who can arrange for safe disposal.

(B) You witness someone who is carrying a weapon into school
Choices:

1. Go up to them and ask them why they have a weapon.
    Putting self at risk. If agitated they could use the weapon on you.

2. Tell a teacher as soon as possible.
   Good move – teacher can then inform others and arrange a suitable course of action to disarm the person.

3. Tell your friends to keep away from them.
   Good move – informing your friends could keep them safe, but this doesn't help anybody else.

4. Authors' suggestion.
   Immediately inform a teacher and ask what else you can do to help.

(C) A friend asks you to look after some cannabis for them
Choices:

1. Take it and then dispose of it.
   By taking possession of the cannabis you may be committing a crime, as is your friend for supplying it to you. Disposing of it may anger your friend.

2. Take it and try some.
   By taking possession of the cannabis, and then trying it, you are committing a crime, as is your friend. Using some of it without the permission of your friend may anger them. The drug may affect you badly.

3. Say that you will not look after it as it is illegal.
   Good move – you are thus keeping yourself safe from a criminal offence and are also informing your friend that what they are doing is illegal.

4. Authors' suggestion.
   Best course of action is 3 above. You may also wish to discuss the dangers of cannabis use with your friend.

(D) Finding a lost and frightened child
Choices:

1. Take them home to your house.
   This could be a good choice if you live nearby and can ask a parent to take charge.

2. Tell them to go to the police.
   Depends on the age of the child, how distressed or frightened they are, and why they are lost. This offers no support.

3. Hand them over to the first adult you see.
   Depends whether you know and can trust the adult.

4. Authors' suggestion.
   Try and calm them, and see if they can give you any information (e.g. name, address, etc.). Stay with them until you can safely hand them to a responsible adult.

(E) Seeing some exposed wires on a damaged lamp post
Choices:

1. Touch it to see if they are live.
   Very dangerous – you could be electrocuted.

2. Try to push the wires back inside.
   Very dangerous – electric shock again possible.

3. Tell a responsible adult who will report it.
   Good move – once reported it could be made safe.

4. Authors' suggestion.
   Best course of action is 3 above. You could monitor the situation to check that it gets fixed.

(F) A friend is offering Ecstasy tablets for sale at school
Choices:

1. Buy some to try.
   Very dangerous – real Ecstasy can kill first time. It is also illegal to possess a class A drug.

2. Warn your other friends not to buy any.
   Good move – shows you care and that you are aware of the danger and illegality.

3. Tell your friend it is illegal to sell drugs.
   Shows you are aware of the law, and that you disapprove of your friend's actions.

4. Authors' suggestion.
   Inform a teacher. They can then take the correct action to ensure that the drugs are taken away and made safe, thus looking after everybody's safety and welfare.

(G) Seeing a person lying by the roadside, looking asleep
Choices:

1. Shake them to try and wake them up.
   Try not to touch them. If they are asleep and woke up startled, they may think they are being attacked and react with violence. If they are injured your shaking may do them even more harm.

2. Call the police or an ambulance on your mobile phone.
   Good move – but, if they are simply asleep, a false alarm.

3. Ignore them because they are probably just drunk.
   They may be ill or so drunk that ignoring them may leave them in serious danger.

4. Authors' suggestion.
    Call to them to see if they respond. If they do, try to ask them how they are. Call for help or get help before doing anything further. If they do not respond call the police or ambulance as 2 above.

(H) Finding a doctor's prescription
Choices:

1. Keep it and try to get it dispensed at a pharmacy.
    This is illegal and you could then be in possession of a potentially dangerous drug.

2. Put it in the waste bin.
    This would be the tidy thing to do, but it doesn't help the person who lost it and who may need the medicines shown on it.

3. Just ignore it and leave it where it is.
    As 2 above – this is irresponsible, and shows a 'don't care attitude'.

4. Authors' suggestion.
    Hand it to a responsible person such as a parent, teacher, pharmacist, policeman, etc. It can then be returned to the rightful owner.

Follow-up exercises

- The situations below could be acted out in role play in group work or presented as the subject of assemblies.

- Participants could be asked to create further realistic scenarios and suggest correct courses of action to be taken.

- Participants could be asked to research similar incidents reported in the media and discuss the actions taken by those involved and the outcomes.

- Contact could be made with the various emergency services to provide up-to-date information and advice.

19.1 Whatever Next?

It seemed too early to get up, and Charlie wished he didn't have to. But today was a school day, and get up he must. He quickly got ready and, after grabbing some toast, said goodbye to his mum and little sister and ran off down the road to school. On his way he passed an old house that some people said was used by local 'druggies' and, as he walked by, he noticed a needle and syringe just by the front door. He looked at it for a while and wondered what to do. **(A)**

As he got nearer to school, he met up with several friends, and they walked along as a noisy group, chatting and laughing. As they neared the school gates, Charlie noticed that one of the older boys who used to bully him, Sasha, was carrying the wooden handle of what looked like a knife, in his left hand, with the blade tucked up into his jacket sleeve. He saw Charlie looking at him and just smiled back. **(B)**

Lessons seemed to go on and on, but eventually it was break time. Charlie met up with his mates once again and they stood around joking and laughing. Then one of Charlie's friends took him to one side saying he had something important to ask him. He told Charlie that his parents were checking on him at home and asked if he could do him a favour. He asked whether Charlie would look after some drugs for him. He told Charlie that it was only cannabis and it would only be for a few days. **(C)**

Back to lessons, French and then maths. Then it was time for lunch, and as Charlie lived so close by, he was able to go home for something to eat. He hadn't gone that far, when he noticed a small boy, possibly only four or five years old, looking very alone and very lost. He went over to the boy who told him he had been playing with friends, but they had run off and left him, and he didn't know where they were, or how to get back home. **(D)**

Lunch came and went, and it was time to return to school. Charlie passed the old house once more, but this time noticed that the lamp post outside had been vandalized and the metal cover over the wires had been broken. Coloured wires were sticking out and looked damaged. He thought this could be a dangerous situation. **(E)**

Charlie liked football, mostly because he was good at it. He was in goal and hadn't let a ball past him all year. A friend of his was standing behind the touchline by the goal post, and mentioned to Charlie that he had something for sale that he might like to try, some pills that make you feel good. He said they were called Ecstasy, and they were going cheap. **(F)**

Geography and history, not Charlie's favourite subjects, came and went very slowly, he thought. Tonight was special, for relatives were coming to dinner, and Charlie's mum had promised to make his favourite meal. He rushed off from school, saying goodbye to his friends, ran up the road by the old house again. At first he thought it was a bundle of old clothes lying on the pavement, but as he got closer, he realized it was actually a person. But were they all right? They appeared to be very still and their eyes were closed. **(G)**

Relatives came, dinner was eaten, and much fun was had by everyone. It was time for Charlie's uncle, aunt and cousins to leave, and he went with them to the front door. Everybody said their goodbyes, and their car moved off. Charlie's mum went back inside, but Charlie stood there waving to his cousins, who he could see in the back window of their car. As he went to turn back inside, he noticed some paper that had been caught in a bush in the garden. He went to retrieve it and, on doing so, he was surprised to find it wasn't just some discarded wrapper, but a fully made out and signed doctor's prescription for a Mr Shah. Charlie did not know a Mr Shah, and the address was not one he knew. **(H)**

Altogether it had been an interesting but tiring day for Charlie, and he was glad to get into bed at last. He lay there thinking about tomorrow, and what he had planned, who he would see, what he would do. Before he knew it, he was fast asleep.

(A) Finding a used and discarded needle and syringe

Choices:

1. Pick it up and put it in the nearest waste bin.
2. Pick it up and put it in your pocket for later.
3. Pick it up and chase your friends with it.
4. None of the above – your suggestion.

(B) You witness someone who is carrying a weapon into school

Choices:

1. Go up to them and ask them why they have a weapon.
2. Tell a teacher as soon as possible.
3. Tell your friends to keep away from them.
4. None of the above – your suggestion.

(C) A friend asks you to look after some cannabis for them

Choices:

1. Take it and then dispose of it.
2. Take it and try some.
3. Say that you will not look after it as it is illegal.
4. None of the above – your suggestion.

(D) Finding a lost and frightened child

Choices:

1. Take them home to your house.
2. Tell them to go to the police.
3. Hand them over to the first adult you see.
4. None of the above – your suggestion.

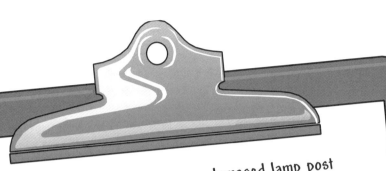

(E) Seeing some exposed wires on a damaged lamp post

Choices:

1. Touch it to see if they are live.
2. Try and push the wires back inside.
3. Tell a responsible adult who will report it.
4. None of the above – your suggestion.

(F) A friend is offering Ecstasy tablets for sale at school

Choices:

1. Buy some to try.
2. Warn your other friends not to buy any.
3. Tell the friend it is illegal to sell drugs.
4. None of the above – your suggestion.

(G) Seeing a person lying by the roadside, looking asleep

Choices:

1. Shake them to try and wake them up.
2. Call the police or an ambulance on your mobile phone.
3. Ignore them because they are probably just drunk.
4. None of the above – your suggestion.

(H) Finding a doctor's prescription

Choices:

1. Keep it and try to get it dispensed at a pharmacy.
2. Put it in the waste bin.
3. Just ignore it and leave it where it is.
4. None of the above – your suggestion.

Exercise 20

Drugs Pyramid Ten

Suggested age: 11–12 • Suggested time: 30–40 minutes

Outline

An exercise to encourage participants to examine pressures, temptations and reasons that lead young people to start or to continue using drugs. It also looks at the corresponding pressures, temptations and reasons that prevent many young people using drugs or that encourage current users to stop.

Purpose and expected outcome

- To enable the examination of issues that affect drug use decisions.
- To place such issues in order of their importance.
- To encourage participants to consider the drug decisions of others.
- To challenge attitudes to drug use.
- To reinforce safety and healthy living messages.

Method

The worksheets should be copied and cut up to produce sufficient sets for small group work. If it is intended to use the sets repeatedly they can be laminated. The teacher or group leader should briefly outline the purpose of the exercise, and split the class up into small groups. The cards that deal with reasons to start or continue drug use should be distributed, one set to each group. Groups should be asked to consider the reasons printed on each card and to select ten of them that, in their opinion, represent the most powerful pressures, temptations or reasons for a young person to start drug use or for an existing user to continue. Each set includes a blank card that can be used by the group to include a reason that they feel has been omitted.

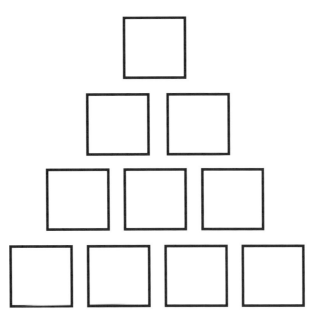

Having selected ten cards the group should then arrange them in the 'pyramid ten' layout, as shown.

The top position should be occupied by the card that, in the opinion of the group, contains the most important and powerful reason to start or continue drug use. The two positions in the second row should be occupied by the cards that contain the next most important or powerful reasons, the third row the three next most important and the bottom row the four cards judged to contain the least important reasons.

When sufficient time has elapsed for each group to arrange its cards in a 'pyramid ten', they should report their choices and placings back to the rest of the class. A simple scoring system can be used to arrive at a common 'pyramid ten'. The card placed at the top by any group should be awarded one point, cards placed in the second row two points, the third row three points and those placed in the bottom row should be awarded four points. Cards not selected for inclusion in any group's 'pyramid ten' should be awarded five points. When all of the groups have reported back, the points can be added up to produce a class 'pyramid ten' shape. The card that scores the lowest number of points should be placed at the top, the next two in the second row and so on until the shape is complete. The two cards that have the highest scores are left out. The teacher can then ask each group why they chose to place a particular card where they did. Groups can also be asked to justify leaving out certain cards or placing them in a lower position. General discussion can then take place.

The cards detailing pressures, temptations and reasons for young people not to start drug use, or for existing users to stop their drug use, can be used in exactly the same way.

This can be used immediately following the previous 'pyramid ten' exercise or on a separate occasion.

Notes for teacher or group leader

Teachers and group leaders should be sensitive to the possibility that some participants may be adversely affected by some statements within this exercise, due to personal experience.

There are no totally right or wrong answers in this exercise. It is an opportunity for participants to discuss their views and, having come to an agreement, indicate their reasoning. Providing the group has given sufficient thought to the placings and are prepared to explain their reasoning, then any placing order is valid. When a group is unable to agree a particular placing, then a simple vote may resolve the dispute. When a dispute is not resolved by voting, then a separate minority placing order may be accepted. Every effort, however, should be made to achieve agreement.

Follow-up exercises

- Creating a set of reasons for becoming involved in other forms of risk taking and anti-social behaviour, e.g. climbing, canoeing, surfing, theft, vandalism and so on.

- Looking at how such pressures, temptations and reasons exert their influence over young people.

20.1 Reasons to Start or Continue Drug Use (1)

To be like
everyone else

The excitement
of risk taking

Everyone is
doing it

Pressure from
friends

Out of curiosity

The thrill
of doing
something illegal

20.1 Reasons to Start or Continue Drug Use (2)

To join in with a group	Nothing much will happen if you get caught
To help forget problems	To have a good time
Because just trying them never hurt anyone	

20.2 Reasons to Stop or Not to Start Drug Use (1)

The death of a friend due to drugs	A girl/boy friend who disapproves
Parents finding out	Getting caught by the police
A bad personal drugs experience	Financial cost

20.2 Reasons to Stop or Not to Start Drug Use (2)

Friends ask you to stop	Health risks
Television reports of drug use	Fear of addiction
Risk to future education and career	

Useful Organizations and Websites

Organizations which offer information, advice and guidance on the teaching of the subjects covered in this workbook:

UK

ASH (Action on Smoking and Health)
Resources and information on smoking education.
102 Clifton Street
London EC2A 4HW
Tel: 020 7739 5902
Website: www.newash.org.uk

Drug Education Forum (DEF)
A forum of national organizations in the UK which offer a service to those who provide drug education to children and young people.
c/o Mentor UK
4th Floor, 74 Great Eastern Street
London EC2A 3JG
Tel: 020 7739 8494
Website: www.drugeducation.forum.com

DrugScope
Formed by the amalgamation of ISDD and SCODA.
Provides expert information, training and resources.
40 Bermondsey Street
London SE1 3UD
Tel: 020 7940 7500
Website: www.drugscope.org.uk

Drug and Alcohol Education and Prevention Team
A joint initiative between DrugScope and Alcohol Concern aiming to identify, develop and promote good practice in alcohol and drug education and prevention.
Tel: 020 7928 1211
Email: ed&prev@drugscope.org.uk

National Health Education Group

A membership group open to professionals whose work has a primary focus of supporting health and/or drugs education with children and young people in formal and informal education settings.
Website: www.nheg.org.uk

TeacherNet

TeacherNet is the government site for teachers. Use this site to access resources, training, professional development and support.
Website: www.teachernet.gov.uk

Teaching Expertise

An organization providing guidance to teachers.
33–41 Dallington Street
London EC1V 0BB
Tel: 0845 450 6404
Website: www.teachingexpertise.com (use site search facility for information about drugs and alcohol teaching)

Australia

REDI (Resistance Education and Drug Information)

A drug information resource for Australian school communities, containing a comprehensive database of information about resources, policies and materials for drug education and incident management.
Website: www.redi.gov.au/default.asp

Canada

D.A.R.E. Canada (Drug Abuse Resistance Education)

Provides resources for teaching and for young people.
Website: www.dare.com/home/default.asp

New Zealand

New Zealand Drug Foundation

Information, resources and links for teachers and others.
PO Box 3082
Wellington
Tel: 4 499 2920 Fax: 4 499 2925
Website: www.nzdf.org.nz/reducing-the-harm

USA

Free (Federal Resources for Educational Excellence)

Teaching and learning resources from federal agencies.
Website: www.free.ed.gov

Organizations which offer resources, information and advice regarding substance misuse:

UK

Alcoholics Anonymous
HQ, PO Box 1, 10 Toft Green
York YO1 7NJ
Tel: 01904 644026 (for local branches consult your telephone directory)
Website: www.alcoholics-anonymous.org.uk

Childline Helpline
0800 11 11 (free, confidential, 24-hour helpline for children in trouble or danger)
Website: www.childline.org.uk

Citizens Advice Bureau
For local branches consult your telephone directory.
Website: www.citzensadvice.org.uk

Connexions Direct
Can help young people with information and advice on issues relating to health.
Tel: 080 800 13219
Website: www.connexions-direct.com

Narcotics Anonymous
UK Service Office
202 City Road
London EC1V 2PH
National help line 020 7730 0009 (10am to 10pm daily)
Website: www.ukna.org (gives details of international contacts)
Email: ukso@ukna.org

National AIDS Trust
New City Cloisters, 196 Old Street
London EC1V 9FR
Tel: 0800 567 123 (24-hour advice and counselling service)
Website: www.nat.org.uk

National Drugs Helpline
Tel: 0800 77 66 00 (free, confidential 24-hour service for users, their families and friends)
Website: www.patient.co.uk/showdoc/26739536
Website designed for young people: www.talktofrank.com

Northern Ireland Council for Voluntary Action
Details of drug services in Northern Ireland.
61 Duncairn Gardens
Belfast BT15 2GB
Tel: 028 9087 7777
Website: www.nicva.org

Parentline Plus
UK registered charity that offers support to anyone parenting a child.
520 Highgate Studios, 53–79 Highgate Road
Kentish Town
London NW5 1TL
Free helpline: 0808 800 2222
Website: www.parentlineplus.org.uk

Rape Crisis
Provides counselling, advice and support to survivors of rape or sexual assault.
Website: www.rapecrisis.org.uk/members.html (gives contact details of local services)

Release
388 Old Street
London EC1V 9LT
Administration tel: 020 7729 5255
Helpline: 0845 4500 215 (24-hour advice, information and referral on legal and drug-related problems for users, their families and friends)
Website: www.release.org.uk

Re-Solv
Works to reduce and prevent solvent abuse.
30a High Street
Stone
Staffordshire ST15 8AW
Tel: 01785 817885
Helpline: 01785 810762 (Mon–Fri 9am to 5pm (answerphone outside these hours); provides confidential service to users, their families and friends)
Website: www.re-solv.org

Samaritans
National lo-call number 08457 90 90 90 (for local branches consult your telephone directory)
Website: www.samaritans.org.uk

Scottish Drugs Forum
Details of drug services in Scotland.
91 Mitchell Street
Glasgow G1 3LN
Tel: 0141 221 1175
Website: www.sdf.org.uk

Australia

National Drugs Strategy Committee
GPO Box 9848
Canberra
ACT2601
Tel: 6 289 7731

Fax: 6 282 5430

Drugs education website: www.dest.gov.au/archive/schools/drugeducation/NSDES.htm

Canada

Canadian Centre on Substance Abuse/National Clearing House on Substance Abuse
Information and advice concerning substance abuse.
112 Kent Street, Site 480
Ottawa KIP 5P2
Tel: 613 235 4048
Website: www.ccsa.ca

Ireland

The Drug Treatment Centre Board
Provides prevention, treatment, rehabilitation and aftercare programmes (in partnership with other agencies).
Trinity Court, 30–31 Pearse Street
Dublin 2
Republic of Ireland
Website: www.addictionireland.ie

The Netherlands

Netherlands Institute of Mental Health and Addiction
Provides advice and literature on drug matters.
PO Box 725
3500 AS Utrecht
Tel: 030 297 11 00 Fax: 030 297 11 11
Website: www.trimbos.nl/default37.html (use site search facility for drugs and alcohol information)

New Zealand

National Society on Alcohol and Drug Dependence (NSAD)
Provides advice and literature on drug matters.
20 Paramoana Street
Ponrua
Tel: 4 237 0273
Website: www.nsad.org.nz

New Zealand Drug Foundation
Provides advice and literature on drug matters.
PO Box 3082
Wellington
Tel: 4 499 2920 Fax: 4 499 2925
Website: www.nzdf.org.nz

USA

National Clearinghouse for Alcohol and Drug Information
Information and advice concerning substance abuse.
Tel: 800 729 6686
Website: http://ncadi.samhsa.gov

Cocaine Helpline
24-hour free and confidential help regarding cocaine use.
Tel: 800 COCAINE (24-hour free and confidential help regarding cocaine use)

National Institute on Drug Abuse
Provides advice and literature on drug matters.
Hotline: 800 662 HELP (24-hour free and confidential help and referral for people with drug problems)
Website: www.nida.nih.gov

For details of other voluntary and statutory agencies in your area that may be able to offer help, advice or information, look in your local telephone directory under 'Help and advice'.

DATE DUE
